# Love, Romance and Intimacy

A Mission 119 Guide to

the Song of Solomon

## Hutson Smelley

Love, Romance and Intimacy

Copyright © 2016 Hutson Smelley

Unless otherwise indicated, Bible quotations are taken from The King James Bible.

Cover art by Dwayne Smith

ISBN: 978-0-9861336-1-9

www.proclaimtheword.me

# Other Works by the Author

Better with Jesus: A Mission 119 Guide to Hebrews (2015)

Chasing Jonah: A Mission 119 Guide to Jonah (2018)

Living Hope: A Mission 119 Guide to First Peter (2019)

Deconstructing Calvinism - Third Edition (2019)

Looking Forward, Living Now: A Mission 119 Guide to Zechariah (2020)

# Table of Contents

# Preface

## Preface to the Mission 119 Series

The psalmist declares, "Thy word is a lamp unto my feet, and a light unto my path." (Psalm 119:105) The Bible is unlike all other books, not only in its grandeur and scope, but because its words are God's Words. The Bible presents to us God's special revelation of Himself, His biased view of history past and future, the reality of who we are, and a picture of all that we can be. Woven within its pages and spilling over is God's redemptive plan for humanity, with Jesus Christ as centerpiece. We do not study the Bible merely to accumulate head knowledge, but with the earnest expectation of knowing God more and drawing near to Him. Each page has something for us, sometimes encouraging us, sometimes reproving us, always revealing God, and every jot and tittle a precious morsel for our souls. Against the backdrop of a world encased in darkness, it is the light of truth that pierces through all the deceptions and puts reality in clear focus.

Every generation faces challenges, and the present generation is challenged about truth and whether any absolute truths are knowable. Like all the ones before it, this generation needs to hear God's Word taught boldly, with clarity, without apology, in grace and love. And this generation needs to be reminded by those who teach that the Bible was written for everyone. God has spoken with clarity so that all believers who come to the Bible yielded to what God has for them can know its truths as they grow and mature. The aim here is to strike the proper balance between too little detail to elucidate the message and superfluous detail that obscures, so that this volume is accessible and profitable to laypersons and teachers alike who seek to understand the author's original intended meaning and the continuing relevance of that message today. With this in mind, the Mission 119 Series is designed to provide guidance for the exposition of books of the Bible with depth and a commitment to a plain sense interpretation tethered first and foremost to the context and flow of argument of the book under consideration before comparison is made to other books and the perceived systematic theology of the Bible. Of a certainty, the Bible has one author and contains neither error nor contradiction, but each of the 66 books and letters in the Bible must be allowed first to speak for itself as the teacher helps learners see the message of the book in context and its application principles.

A common sentiment today is that people need only "relevant" teaching from the Bible, which suggests portions of the Bible are irrelevant, and too often means they want three steps to raising teens in place of the perfections of God, five steps to a better marriage in place of how a believer matures and walks in the Spirit, how to find blessing and wealth in place of God's demand for holy living, and so forth. May I say that every word God ever spoke was relevant and remains so today. Those who would step forward as teachers of the Word of God only do people a disservice by trying to conform God's Holy Word to the world's bankrupt self-help counterfeits when what is most needful today is the plain teaching of the whole Bible as it is. Believers engaged in the Word and yielding to the Holy Spirit will find the most practical of wisdom and grace enablement for all areas of their lives as they draw near to God in the transformative experience of knowing Him more and more. May I also suggest that while some people will flee teaching that has depth and conviction, far more people in churches today are thirsty for more depth in the teaching. They want to see that the Bible is not clichés and recycled sugar sticks but truly a light from God unto their paths. In this vein, it is my prayer that this volume of the Mission 119 Series will be a useful guide for teachers of the Bible and a special blessing for students of the Word who aspire to know God more.

## Preface to Song of Solomon

The Song of Solomon, or Song of Songs (hereafter, the "Song") as it is titled in the first verse of the Song (also called *Canticles* in the Latin), asserts that its author is Solomon: "The song of songs, which is Solomon's." It is widely recognized that the ending of the first verse could be translated to indicate Solomon's authorship or that the Song was written for him or dedicated to him. Notwithstanding, the better view is that the Song is affirmatively claiming Solomon as author because, as will be shown below, Solomon is heralded in the Bible as a gifted songwriter and a man capable of writing the Song, the Song has similarities to other writings of Solomon, and his authorship gives it credibility. It is beyond the scope of this work to provide a thorough biography of the life of Solomon, but it is beneficial to explore his life in some measure in order to answer the question of whether Solomon was capable of writing the Song. It is to that matter that we now turn.

## Life of Solomon

The name "Solomon" means peaceful. He was the second son of King David and Bathsheba. (2 Samuel 12:24) Solomon was born around 990 B.C. He succeeded his father as king and reigned from about 971-931 B.C. The history of Solomon is set forth in 1 Kings 1-11 and 2 Chronicles 1-9. He ultimately reigned for forty years and the nation reached the zenith of its prowess. For after the passing of Solomon, the nation split into northern and southern kingdoms. As David knew his remaining time was limited, he charged Solomon to follow the Lord:

> 1 Kings 2:1 Now the days of David drew nigh that he should die; and he charged Solomon his son, saying, 2 I go the way of all the earth: be thou strong therefore, and shew thyself a man; 3 And keep the charge of the LORD thy God, to walk in his ways, to keep his statutes, and his commandments, and his judgments, and his testimonies, as it is written in the law of Moses, that thou mayest prosper in all that thou doest, and whithersoever thou turnest thyself: 4 That the LORD may continue his word which he spake concerning me, saying, If thy children take heed to their way, to walk before me in truth with all their heart and with all their soul, there shall not fail thee (said he) a man on the throne of Israel.

A life-changing event occurred in Solomon's life early in his reign. God appeared to him and said, "Ask what I shall give thee." (2 Chronicles 1:7) Solomon asked for "wisdom and knowledge, that I may go out and come in before this people: for who can judge this thy people, that is so great?" (2 Chronicles 1:10) God's response was that he would give Solomon the "wisdom and knowledge" as well as wealth and honor:

> 2 Chronicles 1:11 And God said to Solomon, Because this was in thine heart, and thou hast not asked riches, wealth, or honour, nor the life of thine enemies, neither yet hast asked long life; but hast asked wisdom and knowledge for thyself, that thou mayest judge my people, over whom I have made thee king: 12 Wisdom and knowledge *is* granted unto thee; and I will give thee riches, and wealth, and honour, such as none of the kings have had that *have been* before thee, neither shall there any after thee have the like.

What God said he would do, He did in spades. Of Solomon's wealth, we read: "And the king made silver and gold at Jerusalem as plenteous as stones, and cedar trees made he as the sycomore trees that are in the vale for abundance." (2 Chronicles 1:15) His wealth is further recorded in 1 Kings 10, which proclaims: "So Solomon exceeded all the kings of the earth for riches and for wisdom." (1 Kings 10:23) In 1 Kings 4, we have both a description of Solomon's great wisdom as well as his broad knowledge:

> 1 Kings 4:29 And God gave Solomon wisdom and understanding exceeding much, and largeness of heart, even as the

sand that *is* on the sea shore. 30 And Solomon's wisdom excelled the wisdom of all the children of the east country, and all the wisdom of Egypt. 31 For he was wiser than all men; than Ethan the Ezrahite, and Heman, and Chalcol, and Darda, the sons of Mahol: and his fame was in all nations round about. 32 And he spake three thousand proverbs: and his songs were a thousand and five. 33 And he spake of trees, from the cedar tree that *is* in Lebanon even unto the hyssop that springeth out of the wall: he spake also of beasts, and of fowl, and of creeping things, and of fishes. 34 And there came of all people to hear the wisdom of Solomon, from all kings of the earth, which had heard of his wisdom.

Particularly relevant in the quoted passage is Solomon's knowledge of plants, trees and animals, which would be necessary to write the Song with its many allusions to plants, trees, and animals. Also, he is a noted songwriter who composed 1,005 songs.

In addition to being a man of wisdom and knowledge, Solomon was a great builder. King David hoped to build the temple, but ultimately God did not permit it, and instead gave that task to Solomon. David also charged Solomon to build the temple:

1 Chronicles 22:7 And David said to Solomon, My son, as for me, it was in my mind to build an house unto the name of the LORD my God: 8 But the word of the

LORD came to me, saying, Thou hast shed blood abundantly, and hast made great wars: thou shalt not build an house unto my name, because thou hast shed much blood upon the earth in my sight. 9 Behold, a son shall be born to thee, who shall be a man of rest; and I will give him rest from all his enemies round about: for his name shall be Solomon, and I will give peace and quietness unto Israel in his days. 10 He shall build an house for my name; and he shall be my son, and I *will be* his father; and I will establish the throne of his kingdom over Israel for ever. 11 Now, my son, the LORD be with thee; and prosper thou, and build the house of the LORD thy God, as he hath said of thee. 12 Only the LORD give thee wisdom and understanding, and give thee charge concerning Israel, that thou mayest keep the law of the LORD thy God. 13 Then shalt thou prosper, if thou takest heed to fulfil the statutes and judgments which the LORD charged Moses with concerning Israel: be strong, and of good courage; dread not, nor be dismayed.

In addition to building the temple, for instance, Solomon constructed a palace (1 Kings 7:1-12) supported by cedar pillars (the Song will refer to construction using cedars in 1:17). According to his own testimony in Ecclesiastes: "I made me great works; I builded me houses; I planted me vineyards: I made me gardens and orchards and I planted trees in them of all king of fruits: I made me pools of water, to water therewith the wood that bringeth forth trees." (Ecclesiastes 2:4-6) Notably, the Song will frequently make poetic use of the imagery of gardens (4:12, 16; 5:1; 6:2), vineyards (1:6; 7:12), orchards (4:13), trees (2:3), fruits (2:3; 4:16; 8:12), and even pools (7:4) and fountains (4:12, 15). Given Solomon's scientific knowledge combined with his experience building gardens and pools and his talent for songwriting, he plainly had the knowledge and skill necessary to write the Song using the imagery we find there.

## Could Solomon Write the Song?

The next question is whether Solomon could have written the Song in the style in which it is written. "Most scholars who regard the Song as a late work do so primarily because some of the vocabulary found in it appears to be incompatible with the earlier date."[1] These critics argue that the Song contains terms (like loan words from the Greek) indicating a late authorship, even as late as the third century B.C., centuries after Solomon's death. But as Garrett points out, "Linguistic evidence is not conclusive. Attempts to date the book from vocabulary and grammar are inherently weak because of our limited knowledge of the history of the Hebrew language."[2] In addition, there is good reason to reject the linguistic argument:

> These arguments are not as convincing as
> they first appear. The word *parades*

---

[1] Garrett, D. A. (1998), p. 252. Complete citations are in the Select Bibliography.
[2] Garrett, D. A. (1993), p. 349.

("orchard") may come from a Sanskrit root word that is far older than either Persian or Greek. In addition, many words once asserted to be from a late Aramaic background have been found to be more ancient than originally supposed. Also the use of the Hebrew word *she* is not as significant as once was thought. Similar relative pronouns have been found in some ancient Semitic languages, such as Akkadian and Ugaritic. This implies that the use of Hebrew *she* is not an exclusively late phenomenon. In short, the vocabulary of the Song does not prove that it is a late work.[3]

On the other hand, internal evidence supports an early date for the Song. For instance, Song 6:4 references the city Tirzah: "Thou art beautiful, O my love, as Tirzah, comely as Jerusalem, terrible as an army with banners." Garrett explains the significance, from the standpoint of dating the Song, of the reference to Tirzah:

> A particularly significant occurrence of a place name is that of Tirzah in 6:4, where it is set in parallel to Jerusalem. Tirzah was a leading city of the northern part of the nation and capital of the Northern Kingdom until Omri (reigned ca. 885–874 B.C.) built Samaria. The parallelism in 6:4 implies that Tirzah, at the time of composition, was still the chief city of the north. Unless one is willing to beg the

---

[3] Garrett, D. A. (1998), p. 252.

question by asserting that the reference is deliberate archaizing, the implication is that Song of Songs antedates Omri.[4]

The Song likewise references other locations in both the northern (Sharon, Lebanon, Hermon, and Carmel) and southern (Jerusalem and Engedi) portions of Israel, as well as the Transjordan areas of Heshbon and Gilead. "This geographic outlook reflects a time when all Israel was unified and even territories in the Transjordan were under Israelite dominion. These conditions never prevailed after the death of Solomon."[5]

Other internal evidence includes the use of "'single word parallelism' (2:15; 6:8), a feature of late second millennium poetry, [which] is evidence of an early date for the book."[6] And as already noted, Solomon's scientific knowledge base and songwriting skills are consistent with the language of the Song. References to spices likely imported from India also support an early date for the Song.[7] Solomon's reign was a time of great prosperity, and the Song prolifically refers to items usually associated with luxury and wealth that fit an early date best. "Only then did Jerusalem possess the spices, perfumes, and luxuries mentioned in the book as well as great quantities of gold, marble, and precious jewels (Song 5:14–15; see 1 Kings 10:14–22)."[8] The response to the internal evidence by those who hold to a later date is that the poet merely made use for poetic effect of the imagery of more ancient times. The difficulty here is the references

[4] Garrett, D. A. (1993), p. 351.
[5] Garrett, D. A. (1998), p. 252.
[6] Garrett, D. A. (1993), p. 351-52.
[7] Ibid.
[8] Garrett, D. A. (1998), p. 253.

are very specific, indicative of the familiarity inherent in first-hand knowledge. Garrett explains:

> Of course, one can argue that these are only similes and that they do not prove that the writer actually lived in an age when such things were common. It is doubtful, however, that a poet would use imagery, described in such vivid detail, that was outside his own frame of reference. When a poet does venture to use a metaphor that is beyond his personal experience, that metaphor is apt to be of a general nature and ridden with cliché (e.g., "as white as snow" or "as brave as a lion"). Certainly this is not the case in Song of Songs.[9]

## The Parallels to Ancient Egyptian Love Poetry

Perhaps the most compelling of the evidence favoring the early date is solid scholarship showing remarkable parallels between the Song and ancient Egyptian love poetry. According to Garrett: "From Egypt, in the period of approximately 1300 to 1100 B.C., come a number of love songs which are remarkably like Song of Songs. Many of the motifs and ideas that appear in the Song are also found in the Egyptian poetry. Outside of this ancient body of literature, however, it is difficult to find any writings comparable to Song of Songs."[10] Lucas explains: "Since the late 1920s it has been realized that

---

[9] Garrett, D. A. (1993), p. 352.
[10] Garrett, D. A. (1998), p. 253.

the closest parallels to the Song of Songs are to be found in Egyptian love songs that date from *c.* 1300–1150 B.C. There are four different collections of these songs: Chester Beatty Papyrus 1, Papyrus Harris 500, the Turin Papyrus, and the Cairo Love Songs."[11]  While scholars have tried to establish connections with ancient love poetry outside of Egypt, those similarities are far more attenuated:

> In this respect, Egyptian parallels are much closer. The Egyptian love songs are not hymns or liturgies, and they reference gods and cultic activities only incidentally. The lovers are always human, never divine (Fox, *Song of Songs*, 234–35). They are *personae* created by the author as vehicles for speaking poetically about love, romance, and eroticism (Fox, *Song of Songs*, 253–56). Although many parallels exist, they are most strongly expressed in the motif of the praise of the beloved....[12]

Lucas notes a number of the parallels between the Song and ancient Egyptian love poetry:

> There are a number of notable similarities between the Egyptian love songs and the Song of Songs...
>
> • In both the woman is referred to as the 'sister' of her lover. In the Egyptian songs, but not the Song of Songs, the male lover is referred to as 'brother'.

---

[11] Lucas, E. (2003), p. 182.
[12] Jones, C. M. (2015).

- In the Egyptian songs the lovers are presented, or present themselves, in 'fictional roles' as royalty, servant, shepherd. In the Song of Songs they take on the roles of royalty, shepherd, gardener.

- Similar extravagant compliments appear in the Egyptian and Hebrew songs: 'most beautiful youth' / 'fairest among women' (Song 1:8); 'more perfect than the world' / 'my perfect one' (5:2); 'like Sothis [Venus] rising at the beginning of a good year' / '[she comes] forth like the dawn, fair as the moon, bright as the sun' (6:10).

- The descriptions of the beloved in the Egyptian and Hebrew songs use similar comparisons: 'her arms surpass gold' / 'his head is the finest gold' (Song 5:11); 'the mouth of my girl is a lotus bud' / 'his lips are lilies, distilling liquid myrrh' (5:13); 'her breasts are mandrake apples' / 'your two breasts are like two fawns' (7:3).[13]

Of course, there are differences as well, but these are consistent with the Hebrew style of poetry. For instance, "[a] striking difference between the Egyptian songs and the Song of Songs is that whereas there is a genuine dialogue between the lovers in the Song of Songs, the Egyptian songs are soliloquies in which speakers address their own hearts."[14] Further, "[i]n a detailed study of Egyptian love poetry and the Song,

---

[13] Lucas, E. (2003), pp. 182-83.
[14] Ibid., pp. 183-84.

13

however, Fox has noted that the Song is much more unified than any simple grouping of Egyptian love lyrics. We agree that the refrains and repeated expressions in the Song ('I adjure you ... not to arouse love,' 'I am my beloved's and he is mine'), the common themes ('seek' and 'find'), the common time frame (spring), the sequencing between units, and the consistent character portrayal do point to a more structured work."[15]

To give a (by no means exhaustive) sense of the close parallels between the Song and ancient Egyptian love poetry, below is a sampling from Egyptian poems and citations to verses within the Song that use similar imagery. First are examples from The Love Songs of Papyrus Harris 50, which date from the 10th and 11th centuries B.C.[16]

> (compare to Song 8:14)
> Make haste to see your beloved,
> Like a horse in the open field,
> Like a falcon [diving down] to its reeds.

> (compare to Song 4:12, 16; 5:1; 7:7-8, 13)
> [How] intoxicating are the plants of my garden!
> [The lips] of my beloved are the bud of a lotus,
> Her breasts are mandrakes.

> (compare to Song 5:7)
> Though I be beaten and driven off

---

[15] Ogden, G. S., & Zogbo, L. (1998), p. 5.
[16] Simpson, William Kelly (2003), pp. 308-33. All of the quotes from the Egyptian love poems are taken from this source.

To dwell in the Delta marshes,
(Driven) to the land of Khor with sticks and clubs,
To the land with switches of palm,
To the high ground with rods,
Or to the low ground with branches.
I will pay no heed to their warnings
To abandon the one whom I desire.

(compare to Song 8:2)
Sweet pomegranate wine in my mouth
Is like the bitter gall of birds.

(compare to Song 2:4)
You have spread your love (over me).

(compare to Song 4:12-14)
I am your first beloved;
I belong to you like a plot of land
Which I have made to bloom
With flowers and every sweet herb.

The stanza below is from The Cairo Love Songs, which date to the 11th, 12th or 13th centuries.

(compare to Song 8:6)
Would that I were her signet ring
Which is upon her finger,
For I would see her love every day,
And it would be I who would touch her heart.

Next are lines from The Love Songs of Papyrus Chester Beatty, dating from the 12<sup>th</sup> century B.C.

> (compare to Song 2:2; 6:9-10)
> My beloved is unrivaled,
> There is none equal to her,
> She is beautiful beyond all women.

> (compare to Song 4:4; 5:14; 7:4)
> High is her neck,
> Resplendent are her breasts,
> Of pure lapis lazuli is her hair.
> Her arms surpass (even) gold,
> Like lotus flowers are her fingers.

> (compare to Song 8:1)
> I shall kiss him in the presence of his family
> And not be embarrassed by the people.

> (compare to Song 5:2-8)
> It is seven days yesterday that I have not seen my beloved!
> Affliction has spread throughout me,
> My limbs have become heavy,
> And I have forgotten my own body.

Finally, below is a stanza from the Nakht-Sobek Songs from Papyrus Chester Beatty, also from the 12<sup>th</sup> century B.C.

(compare to Song 4:9; 6:5; 8:6)
How skilled is my beloved in throwing the snare,
Although a breeder of cattle did not beget her.
With her tresses she throws the snare at me,
With her eyes she entraps me,
With her necklace she binds me,
And with her signet ring she brands me.

As shown above, the parallels between the Song and ancient Egyptian poetry are considerable. A natural question is whether those parallels make sense if Solomon were the author of the Song. Duane Garrett explains why the parallels are unsurprising:

> What is the reason for this unusual parallel between a book of the Bible and Egyptian poetry? Solomon made an alliance with the Egyptian Pharaoh and married his daughter (1 Kings 3:1). The court of Solomon and Egypt doubtless had extensive contacts. Solomon also had contact with wise men—and thus their literature—from all over the world (1 Kings 4:29–34).
>
> Solomon likely would have become familiar with the love poetry that had appeared within the previous three hundred years in Egypt. This would explain how the Song has so much in common with its Egyptian counterparts. Solomon, after all, was cosmopolitan in his learning and tastes.[17]

---

[17] Garrett, D. A. (1998), p. 253.

Of course, if the Song were written centuries later as critical scholars maintain, the parallels to ancient Egyptian poetry are inexplicable. In summary, based on the internal and external evidence, we may conclude: "The poetry of Song of Songs reflects Solomon's age better than any other of Israelite history. It is thus best to assume it was written in that period."[18]

## Interpreting the Song

Beyond the question of whether Solomon credibly wrote the Song is the question of how to interpret it. Surely no other book of the Bible is quite like the Song, nor does any have as many varied interpretations. And notably, there is no clear reference to God in the Song, although arguably God is referenced in Song 8:6. Notwithstanding the Song's not mentioning God explicitly, the famous Jewish Rabbi Akiba said: "the whole world is not worth the day on which the Song of Songs was given to Israel; all the Writings are holy, and the Song of Songs is the holy of holies." Some of the more popular theories of interpretation are as follows:

1. The allegorical method was popular both in ancient Israel and later among early Christians and persists in different forms to this day. Historically, this has been the most popular approach to the book. In this view, the erotic language of the Song is actually an allegory for the relationship between God and Israel, or between Jesus and the Church. For instance, some would argue that Shulamite represents the virgin Mary and Solomon

---

[18] Ibid.

represents Jesus. This interpretational approach solves some "problems" in that once the "Solomon" in the Song represents God, the Song is no longer subject to criticism for not referencing God. Also, many have insisted God would not inspire a writing about sexual love, which the allegorical view does away with. Indeed, the Song "...contains a number of erotic verses and for this reason, it is said that rabbis were once forbidden to read it until they were thirty years old."[19] The problems with the allegorical view are, first, that there is no indication in the text that it is to be understood as an allegory, nor any sure means to establish what the supposed symbols mean. Invariably, the reader interprets the allegory to suit his bias, giving the Song an arbitrary interpretation not susceptible to objective testing. Second, the language is too erotic for the allegorical interpretations most often proposed. The Song does not simply show a relationship between a man and a woman that plausibly could picture the relationship between Christ and the Church (see Ephesians 5:32). Instead, the Song speaks in intimate terms of foreplay and lovemaking that do not seem to fit anything the New Testament says about Jesus and the Church.

2. Similar to the allegorical method is the typical method. This view understands the Song literally but then also seeks a second, spiritualized meaning, usually to refer to the relationship between Jesus and all believers. But the same criticisms of the allegorical method apply here. In addition, it does not seem plausible that the original audience could have possibly understood the Song in this way.

---

[19] Water, M. (1998), p. 22.

3. Another popular view is the dramatic interpretation, which views the Song as a drama either involving two or three main characters. In the two-character approach, there is a love affair between Solomon and the young maiden Shulamite. In the three-character approach, Solomon has taken Shulamite away to marry her, stealing her from her shepherd lover. Thus, some of the lines in the Song are attributed to Solomon, and others to the unnamed shepherd. However, there are no indications in the Song that it is a drama such as dramatic instructions, nor is there good evidence to support that such dramas existed in ancient Israel at the time Solomon could have authored the work. Further, a drama conveys a story, but the Song at best has elements of a story. The Song conveys a few events such as the courtship, the wedding feast, and the consummation of the wedding, but it lacks the elements of a plot, an antagonist, or an ending. Also, the Song is not strictly chronological as we would expect of a drama.

4. Another view is that the Song is a collection of love poems not necessarily connected, with different sections having different authors. The notes to the text of the Song in the chapters that follow will argue for the unity of the Song. The evidence for this unity is substantial, thus making this view improbable. Moreover, without that unity, then it is difficult to discern any central message of the Song justifying the view that it is inspired Scripture, "profitable for doctrine, for reproof, for correction, for instruction in righteousness." (2 Timothy 3:16)

5. The approach taken in this book is that the Song is, as its opening verse states, a "song." It is Hebrew poetry

within the genre of a song, and should be interpreted as poetry. This allows for a literal interpretation—that the Song really is about two lovers getting married and having sex—while also giving effect to the figures of speech and figurative language common to Hebrew poetry. This is the preferred view for the following additional reasons: (i) the Song claims to be a "song"; (ii) this view makes sense of the Song's repetition of both words and themes; (iii) this view accounts for the Song's lack of all the elements of a story; (iv) this view allows for the fact that the Song is not strictly chronological; and (v) this view emphasizes the unity of the Song. Moreover, this view is supported by the Song's parallels to Egyptian love poetry: "The Song of Songs belongs to the genre of love poetry— a genre well-attested in both Mesopotamian and Egyptian literature. Strong parallels between Egyptian love songs and the biblical Song of Songs suggest that the Song was originally composed as a series of dramatic vignettes to be sung for entertainment at festive occasions."[20]

## Why Study the Song?

Perhaps the larger question than how to interpret the Song is the "so what?" question. Why should Christians bother reading a 3,000 year old love song? And does the Song add anything that we do not otherwise obtain elsewhere from the Bible. As some are quick to point out, the Song does not even explicitly reference God. Answering that charge, one commentary succinctly explains: "Although Song of Songs contains no explicit

---

[20] Jones, C. M. (2015).

reference to God, like the book of Esther (which also doesn't directly reference God), Song of Songs is full of God's presence. Throughout the book, we see reflections on God's creation—and him working through the romance of these two people."[21] To that we may add that much of wisdom literature (e.g., Proverbs, Ecclesiastes) does not directly reference God, yet interpreting the Song as a song, it becomes apparent that the Song is wisdom literature. The central teaching is repeated three times—that sexual conduct should be reserved for the right person within the context of marriage. (Song 2:7, 3:5, 8:4) "Despite there being a wide range of interpretations of Song of Songs, it's clear that the book celebrates human sexuality and advocates for experiencing it with all of our senses—from the Bible's larger perspective, this happens in the context of marriage."[22] Garrett explains the overall message of the Song: "The message is that the mutual pleasures of love are good and possible even in this fallen world. The Song is a testimony to the grace of God and a rejection of *both* asceticism and debauchery."[23]

What the Song adds to the Biblical corpus of teaching about marriage and sexuality is that one of the God-ordained purposes of sex is pleasure. "God is the giver of all good things, including sex."[24] "In Proverbs we find a picture of faithful love, and the injunction to 'rejoice in the wife of your youth' (Proverbs 5:18). The joy and pleasure of marriage and sexuality—as God ordered it at

---

[21] Barry, J. D., Mailhot, J., Bomar, D., Ritzema, E., & Sinclair-Wolcott, C. (Eds.). (2014).

[22] Ibid.

[23] Garrett, D. A. (1993), p. 380.

[24] Water, M. (1998), p. 22.

creation—finds its expression in Song of Songs (Genesis 2:24–25)."[25] Further, while much of what is stated outside the Song is in the form of commands and prohibitions, the Song argues from the perspective of wisdom—that the blessing available in following the wisdom of God exceeds the experience to be obtained in rejecting it. Commentator Duane Garrett explains the value of the Song to the greater picture of sexuality in the Bible:

> Love and sexuality can be a source of great joy or deep grief and pain. As children become adults and discover their sexuality, and as couples move into marriage and seek to understand each other, it is imperative that they have guidance in this area of life that is so crucial to psychological adjustment. The Bible itself would be incomplete if it only spoke of sexuality in terms of prohibitions and did not give positive instruction to enable the reader to discover the joy of healthy love. Certainly love between man and woman is not the whole of life or even its highest good. The Bible elsewhere emphasizes the vertical relationship between a man or a woman and God as more important than any other. Even so, to regard Song of Songs as unworthy of canonization unless it is allegorized or turned into a historical drama is to deny the crucial importance of cherishing and understanding this area of

---

[25] Barry, J. D., Mailhot, J., Bomar, D., Ritzema, E., & Sinclair-Wolcott, C. (Eds.). (2014).

life. It also reflects a failure to appreciate the place of wisdom literature as a guide to healthy and happy behavior in this world.[26]

Finally, it is worth noting that the Song provides a powerful picture of sexuality through God's eyes that is a far cry from the distorted view given by secular culture and especially modern entertainment. "In a culture that distorts sexuality—and exploits it for profit and selfish pleasure—we need Song of Songs to affirm the value of sexuality in marriage, which is further sanctioned and redeemed by the work of Jesus. The beautiful images in Song of Songs show us that love and sexuality can be good and pure—an alternative to the broken-heartedness, distortion, and violence of our culture."[27] Other important subthemes include affection, the emotions prior to the wedding, healthy communications in a marriage, and protecting the purity of others.

## The Outline of the Song

Key to interpreting any book of the Bible is grasping the "big picture" of the book. For this reason, I highly recommend that you read the Song through several times before engaging in this study, paying special attention to words and ideas that are emphasized or repeated, as well as those words and ideas that suggest a unity to the Song. As we interpret, we must seek to do so within the immediate and greater context of each passage, as well as interpreting in light of the overall argument or purpose of

[26] Garrett, D. A. (1993), pp. 367-68.
[27] Barry, J. D., Mailhot, J., Bomar, D., Ritzema, E., & Sinclair-Wolcott, C. (Eds.). (2014).

the book. We must remain mindful that we are reading Hebrew poetry about love and romance, and not a modern "how to" manual. To this end, an outline of the Song is provided below:

1. INTRODUCTION (1:1)
2. WEDDING DAY (1:2-2:7)
   a. Wedding night anticipation (1:2-4)
   b. Resentment of Shulamite's brothers (1:5-6)
   c. Searching for Solomon (1:7-8)
   d. Praise for Shulamite's beauty (1:9-11)
   e. Wedding night anticipation (1:12-14)
   f. Praise for Shulamite's beauty (1:15)
   g. The season for love (1:16-17)
   h. A common Shulamite (2:1)
   i. An uncommon Shulamite (2:2)
   j. An uncommon Solomon (2:3)
   k. Wedding night anticipation (2:4-6)
   l. First charge to the daughters (2:7)
3. COURTSHIP (2:8-3:5)
   a. The seasons change (2:8-14)
   b. Shulamite's invitation to Solomon (2:15-17)
   c. Searching for Solomon (3:1-4)
   d. Second charge to the daughters (3:5)
4. MARITAL UNION (3:6-5:1)
   a. Narrator announces Solomon (3:6-11)
   b. Solomon's answer to Shulamite's invitation (4:1-7)
   c. Solomon's invitation to Shulamite (4:8-15)
   d. Marriage consummated (4:16-5:1)

5. MARITAL JITTERS (5:2-6:9)

    a. Searching for Solomon (5:2-8)

    b. Shulamite defends her uncommon Solomon (5:9-16)

    c. Solomon enters the garden (6:1-3)

    d. Praise for Shulamite's beauty (6:4-9)

6. MARRIED LIFE EMBRACED (6:10-8:4)

    a. Narrator announces Shulamite (6:10)

    b. Shulamite enters the garden (6:11-12)

    c. Daughter seeks Shulamite's return (6:13A)

    d. Solomon expresses their union (6:13B-7:9A)

    e. Shulamite expresses their union (7:9B-8:3)

    f. Third charge to the daughters (8:4)

7. CONCLUSION (8:5-14)

    a. Narrator announces the couple (8:5A)

    b. Praise for their love (8:5-7)

    c. Appreciation for Shulamite's brothers (8:8-12)

    d. Solomon's invitation (8:13)

    e. Shulamite's invitation (8:14)

## A Word About Translations

A final note about interpreting the Song is that you will find considerable variation at places among the popular translations if you compare them. As one commentator explains, one reason for this is the unique language employed in the Song: "One of the major problems in translating the Song of Songs is the fact that in its 117 verses there are 47 words (some of them occurring only once) that do not appear elsewhere in the Hebrew Bible.

This makes discerning their meaning difficult."[28] On the other hand, the evidence shows that the text of the Song has been well preserved: "The Hebrew text of the Song of Songs has been well preserved. Four manuscripts of the book have been found at Qumran (4QCant[a,b,c,] 6QCant), all dating from between 30 B.C. and A.D. 70. Of these 4QCant[a] and 4QCant[b] contain a considerable portion of the text. In general they support what is now the traditional Hebrew text, the Massoretic Text (MT)."[29] In this commentary, we follow the King James Version not only because it is a solid translation, but also because it has an elegance befitting the Song and a fairly literal approach to the translation. A complete copy of the Song can be found in Appendix A. Do be aware, however, that many modern translations indicate a "speaker" for the lines of the Song. While these markers may be helpful, they are translators' notes and not part of the original text. In the chapters that follow, the speakers are marked, but again, those attributions are my opinion only and you will find variations of opinions in places as to who is speaking. Just as with the interpretation of any given verses, context is key to understanding who is speaking.

[28] Lucas, E. (2003), p. 178.
[29] Ibid.

# Chapter 1

# The Most Awesome Song

We have a rarely used English term *polymath* that means "a person of great learning in several fields of study." This is someone skilled in several fields or disciplines that may include sciences, literature and various arts. The term derives from the Greek *polymathēs*, which means "having learned much." In the modern vernacular, we call such a person a "Renaissance man." Examples of polymaths include Plato (428/427-348/347 B.C.; philosophy, science, mathematics), Aristotle (384-322 B.C.; biology, ethics, logic, metaphysics, poetry, politics, rhetoric, zoology), Archimedes (287-212 B.C.; astronomy, engineer, inventor, mathematics, physics, philosophy), and Leonardo da Vinci (A.D. 1452-1519; inventions, botany, geology, zoology, painter, sculptor, architect, engineer). The often overlooked Renaissance man, and the greatest of them all, was Solomon, whom God specially imbued with diverse skills in literature, science and wisdom:

> 1 Kings 4:29 And God gave Solomon wisdom and understanding exceeding

much, and largeness of heart, even as the sand that *is* on the sea shore. 30 And Solomon's wisdom excelled the wisdom of all the children of the east country, and all the wisdom of Egypt. 31 For he was wiser than all men; than Ethan the Ezrahite, and Heman, and Chalcol, and Darda, the sons of Mahol: and his fame was in all nations round about. 32 And he spake three thousand proverbs: and his songs were a thousand and five. 33 And he spake of trees, from the cedar tree that *is* in Lebanon even unto the hyssop that springeth out of the wall: he spake also of beasts, and of fowl, and of creeping things, and of fishes. 34 And there came of all people to hear the wisdom of Solomon, from all kings of the earth, which had heard of his wisdom.

Each polymath has some pinnacle artistic, literary or scientific achievement. Leonardo da Vinci had his *Mona Lisa*. And Solomon, with his tremendous wisdom and skills given to him by God, had his song *par excellence*, what we refer to as Solomon's Song of Songs, or the Song of Solomon. If Solomon had a *Mona Lisa*, the Song of Songs was it. This was his very best of the 1,005 songs he wrote. The subject matter of the Song of Songs is love, romance and sex within a marriage context. If Solomon's wisdom excelled all others, and the Bible affirms that to be the case, then the Song has something for us about this crucial matter in our lives. It is not a message of commands and prohibitions, but of beauty and wisdom.

## Scripture And Comments

<u>Song 1:1</u> The song of songs, which *is* Solomon's.

The Bible records of **Solomon** that "he spake three thousand proverbs: and his songs were a thousand and five." We have little today of those 1,005 songs. In the Psalter, we have only Psalm 127 specifically attributed to Solomon, and then we have **the song of songs** also attributed to **Solomon**. Some would argue that the phrase **song of songs** indicates a collection of songs, but it seems better to understand the inscription here to mean that of all **Solomon's** 1,005 songs, this is the crown jewel or, as noted in the introduction, his song *par excellence* as the translation notes to the NET translation indicate. Similar expressions in the Bible are "holy of holies" (Hebrews 9:3), "vanity of vanities" (Ecclesiastes 1:1), and "king of kings and Lord of Lords" (Revelation 19:16). What we know of Solomon suggests he was a Renaissance man and one of the literary giants of the ancient world. That this work should not only be preserved by God's good hand, but also singled out as Solomon's crown jewel of **songs** should come as little surprise in view of the subject matter. For God created marriage as part of His creative masterpiece during the six days: "Therefore shall a man leave his father and his mother, and shall cleave unto his wife: and they shall be one flesh." (Genesis 2:24) While the Bible elsewhere addresses sex, only here are romance and sexual pleasure within marriage addressed in detail from the standpoint of its beauty and pleasure. The sufficiency of the Bible for our Christian lives could hardly be asserted without the **song of songs**.

As indicated in the preface, there is no sufficient reason to doubt Solomon's authorship, or that such a work could have been created during the time in which Solomon lived given the noted parallels to contemporaneous Egyptian love poetry. Moreover, the **song** is often viewed as a collection of separate works, but as the exegesis that follows will demonstrate, the well-unified nature of the **song of songs** weighs heavily in favor of it being a single unified work with a unified purpose. Finally, the term **song** need not necessarily mean that the work was intended to be sung aloud as opposed to love poetry to be read aloud. What is key is that the work claims for itself to be a **song**, and this should guide our interpretation.

SHULAMITE

Song 1:2 Let him kiss me with the kisses of his mouth:

for thy love *is* better than wine.

3 Because of the savour of thy good ointments

thy name *is as* ointment poured forth,

therefore do the virgins love thee.

4 Draw me, we will run after thee:

the king hath brought me into his chambers:

Note that I indicated above that this portion of the Song represents the words of the lead female speaker, identified in Song 6:13 as "Shulamite." But understand that the Hebrew text does not identify the speaker for each verse, nor when the speaker changes. We are left to determine from what is said, and from the context, who the speaker is, and in that regard there are places where the speaker is plain to see and others where the identification of the speaker may be debated. Many newer translations identify the speaker of each line of the Song, but those are only the editors' viewpoints and not all of the newer translations are in accord as to who is speaking in each line. To make it more confusing, those who view there being more than one male character (e.g., Solomon and another lover) will naturally attribute the lines differently than those who see only one male character. The view taken here is that there is only one male lover.

While the Song is neither a fully developed story nor a drama, we will see as it unfolds that the Song relates a sequence (not necessarily chronologically) of events through different speakers. This sequence relates a man and woman who engage in a courtship, then marry and experience bliss in their lovemaking. What is striking throughout is that while the male lover is certainly critical to the Song, it is written from Shulamite's viewpoint with an emphasis on her anticipation, her emotions (including fear or trepidation), her sexual experience, and her wisdom for other young ladies who look for their Solomon. The Song conveys her reflections on her experiences during courtship, the long-awaited wedding and physical consummation, the rite of passage as she leaves behind childhood to be a wife, and romance after the wedding. Shulamite heralds nothing of the modern historical caricature of love and marriage in the ancient world where women were property and sex was solely for the man's good pleasure and reproduction. We know those abuses existed and still do, but they are foreign to the Song. In Shulamite, we will see inner and outer beauty, assertiveness, initiative, mystery, purity, spontaneity, strength, and wisdom. And so it is from the beginning of the Song that she takes the lead in setting up what is to come.

These opening lines are best viewed as a summary reflection of Shulamite's anticipation of and the consummation of her marriage. This tells us plainly that this is a song of physical romance. These lines will be followed by a response from what we might refer to as the "chorus" or the "daughters of Jerusalem" (more notes on that below), with whom Shulamite will interact throughout the Song, for prior to her marriage she was one of those "daughters," and it is to them that her wisdom on marriage and sexuality is addressed.

Shulamite's opening line draws us into her reflection with the words, **let him kiss me with the kisses of his mouth**. Much of the Song will show the two lovers' anticipation of their physical union, and this is the theme introduced in this first line. She is a passionate woman and what she anticipates (**let him**) is not abuse or mere "wifely duties" but mutual physical enjoyment of their expressed passions for one another. The explicit identification of her lover as Solomon occurs first in 3:9. The **kisses of his mouth** she longs for is the prelude or foreplay to their first sexual encounter. In the next line she says, **for thy love is better than wine**. Note here the change from third person (**let him**) to second person (**for thy**). This is a common device in the ancient writings. The term **love** is the Hebrew *dod*, which Strong's states is "from an unused root meaning properly, to boil, i.e. (figuratively) to love; by implication, a love-token, lover, friend; specifically an uncle:--(well-)beloved, father's brother, love, uncle." While the term is often translated "uncle," it takes on the sense of lovemaking when used in a sexual context as it is often used in the Song:

> Proverbs 7:18 Come, let us take our fill of **love** until the morning: let us solace ourselves with loves.

Ezekiel 16:8 Now when I passed by thee, and looked upon thee, behold, thy time *was* the time of **love**; and I spread my skirt over thee, and covered thy nakedness: yea, I sware unto thee, and entered into a covenant with thee, saith the Lord GOD, and thou becamest mine.

Ezekiel 23:17 And the Babylonians came to her into the bed of **love**, and they defiled her with their whoredom, and she was polluted with them, and her mind was alienated from them.

Shulamite compares Solomon's **love** to **wine**. The Hebrew term *yayin* translated wine means fermented wine, as is apparent from its use in verses like Genesis 9:21 ("and he drank of the wine, and was drunken"). The point then is that while wine has intoxicating effects to the body that some would view as pleasurable, his lovemaking brings **better** physical pleasure to the whole body. The term will be used again in Song 2:4, 4:10, 5:1, 7:9, and 8:2 as with several other recurring elements throughout the Song. Indeed, in 4:10, Solomon will tell her, "how much better is thy love than wine." The recurring elements act as connection points unifying the Song. What may strike us as odd is that the first line rings of anticipation and yet the second line of past experience. But we must remember that the entire Song reflects back on prior events leading to and beyond the consummation of their marriage. Here, Shulamite reflects on her anticipation of the event from the vantage of having already experienced it.

Shulamite continues by praising the great qualities of her lover, explaining that **because of the savour of** Solomon's **good ointments** his **name is as ointment poured forth**.

What Shulamite does here is reflect on his **savour** (fragrance) as a result of his **good ointments** or fine colognes. But the physical fragrance from Solomon's colognes pictures the nature of his personal reputation. Just as when the bottle of colognes is **poured forth** and the fragrance would fill a room, so also her lover's **name** or reputation has spread in the community **as ointment poured forth**. Throughout the Song, Shulamite will articulate his qualities, both physical qualities and other qualities, so that here she can speak of his good **name**. Shulamite illustrates the sort of reverence or respect for her lover that Paul speaks of in Ephesians 5:33 as appropriate for a wife toward her husband. As she contemplates these qualities, she concludes, **therefore do the virgins love thee**. The point is that it is no surprise, in view of his fine qualities, that he enjoys the admiration of the **virgins**. As the Song unfolds, the **virgins** will be identified as the "daughters of Jerusalem." (See, e.g., Song 1:5, 2:7, 3:5, 3:10, 5:8, 5:16, 8:4) The term **virgin** is the Hebrew *almah* and means here a young woman of a marriageable age. The "daughters of Jerusalem" will be sometimes referred to in the notes as the "chorus" as they will interact with Shulamite in one accord, and it is to this group of young ladies that Shulamite belongs before her transition to the role of a wife and lover.

Just as Shulamite longed for her lover to **kiss** her with the **kisses of** his **mouth**, she also longed for him to **draw** her to the bedroom. Though she longs with great anticipation to make love to him, she looks to him to take the initiative, only at the proper time, of wooing her to the bedroom. She says, **we will run after thee**, expressing a sense of urgency, essentially a plea to make haste (cf. 8:14). She then states that **the king hath**

**brought me into his chambers**. Note that it is possible to translate this phrase in the sense of "oh that the king would bring me....", again emphasizing anticipation. But the KJV makes more sense here since Shulamite already commented that "thy love [lovemaking] is better than wine" and it is more consistent with the chorus' response addressed below. Again, she reflects on the anticipation she had prior to their wedding night from the vantage point of looking back. She was eager for the moment when Solomon would **draw** her to his bedroom to make love to her for the first time. Also, here, as elsewhere in the Song, her lover is referred to as the king (Song 1:12, 3:9, 3:11 and 7:5), and elsewhere will be referred to by name as Solomon (Song 3:9, 3:11, 8:11-12).

There is considerable debate as to whether the intent of the Song is that her lover is literally King Solomon (in other words, whether the Song is based on historical events) or Solomon is only being used as a sort of poetic device. A song need not relate historical events. We do not have confirmation outside the Song that anything recorded within actually occurred, and attempts to argue from outside the Song that Shulamite was one of Solomon's hundreds of wives are more driven by a bias toward establishing the Song's historicity than the textual evidence. This silence, though surprising if the Song actually related history, does not conclusively prove that the events did not occur. The point, however, is that in the genre of love poetry and love songs, just as in modern love songs within our culture, they relate events nearly always in order to convey the emotions associated with those events and not to record history. Consider the following lyrics from Elvis Presley's "Heartbreak Hotel":

Well, since my baby left me
Well, I found a new place to dwell
Well, it's down at the end of Lonely Street
At Heartbreak Hotel
Where I'll be, I'll be so lonely, baby
Well, I'm so lonely
I'll be so lonely, I could die
*   *   *

Now, the bell hops tears keep flowin'
And the desk clerk's dressed in black
Well, they've been so long on Lonely Street
Well, they'll never, they'll never look back
And they'll be so, where they'll be so lonely, baby
Well, they're so lonely
They're so lonely, they could die

When we hear Elvis' famous hit song, which he sings in the first person as if he actually experienced the events, we do not assume any history is being relayed. We do not assume that Elvis is singing of a real relationship, nor that upon the breakup he went to stay at a real hotel called "Heartbreak Hotel," nor even that he actually observed bell hops in tears and the clerk in black clothes. We also do not understand him to be saying he is literally about to die. Rather, we understand all of the imagery to convey very beautifully the emotion of loneliness after the breakup. But this illustrates the problem associated with assuming the Song relays history and with giving too literal an interpretation of the Song so that we find ourselves arguing that the "Heartbreak Hotel" is an actual hotel. In any event, regardless of whether the Song is understood to relate historical events or not, it need not affect the overall message and wisdom of the Song.

DAUGHTERS

we will be glad and rejoice in thee,

we will remember thy love more than wine:

As indicated already, the chorus will interact with Shulamite throughout the Song. Here, in response to Shulamite's exclamation that the king brought her to his bedroom, the chorus says, **we will be glad and rejoice in thee**. Again, the chorus refers to the young single ladies of Jerusalem of a marriageable age (sometimes referred to as the virgins), but used here almost like a fictional "character" (and really, a poetic device), not only to interact with Shulamite but to transition between the various reflections in the Song and provide an audience within the Song for Shulamite's wisdom. Shulamite was a member of this group of young ladies, but no longer after her wedding night. The chorus to which she previously was a part gives approval to the relationship Shulamite has with her husband and their mutual enjoyment of one another. The chorus will honor that intimacy, saying **we will remember thy love** (again, read "lovemaking") **more than wine**. Shulamite commented that their experience of physical intimacy was more "intoxicating" than any wine, which proposition the chorus now acknowledges and confirms. In so doing, the fictional "daughters of Jerusalem" give acknowledgement to the high value of what Shulamite and Solomon have in their relationship. Ultimately, it will be to the "daughters of Jerusalem" that Shulamite issues instruction on the importance of waiting for the right person and the right time to enjoy intimacy within the context of marriage. Here, the Song sets the context for Shulamite to share her learned wisdom later as the chorus witnesses and acknowledges that what Shulamite and her lover have is of great value, justifying the wait.

SHULAMITE

the upright love thee.

Shulamite responds to the words of the chorus, in reference to her lover, that **the upright love thee**. The term **love** here is not the same Hebrew word spoken by the chorus when they said in reference to lovemaking, "we will remember thy love more than wine." Rather, the idea here is that of adoration. Shulamite's response to the chorus, then, is that the chorus is correct or right (or **upright**) to adore **thee**, that is, to adore her lover.

SHULAMITE

5 I *am* black, but comely,

O ye daughters of Jerusalem,

as the tents of Kedar,

as the curtains of Solomon.

6 Look not upon me, because I *am* black,

because the sun hath looked upon me:

my mother's children were angry with me;

they made me the keeper of the vineyards;

*but* mine own vineyard have I not kept.

7 Tell me, O thou whom my soul loveth,

where thou feedest,

where thou makest *thy flock* to rest at noon:

for why should I be as one that turneth aside

by the flocks of thy companions?

As Shulamite contemplates her upcoming wedding, she is self-conscious about her physical appearance and articulates her inner feelings to the chorus: **I am black, but comely, O ye daughters of Jerusalem**. As verse 6 will make clear, her use of the term **black** means dark or tanned, which she attributes to the fact that **the sun hath looked upon me**. Indeed, she attributes the ultimate cause of her darkened complexion to **my mother's children**, meaning her brothers, as will become apparent in the final chapter of the Song, because they **were angry with** her and **made her the keeper of the vineyards**. In other words, as Shulamite reflects back on her self-conscious feelings, she recalls placing blame on her brothers for forcing her to work outside in the family business, namely maintaining and harvesting **the vineyards**. We will see in chapter 8 that Shulamite will come to terms with her feelings toward her brothers' actions and view those actions as their means of protecting her purity. In any event, as a result of her laboring in the elements as a **keeper of the** literal **vineyards**, she was unable tend to her **own** figurative **vineyard**, meaning her physical body. Here, as throughout the Song, her physical body will be portrayed with imagery of flowers, gardens, and vegetation.

We need to recognize that Shulamite's feelings are balanced. She views herself as **comely** or beautiful and yet at the same time she is troubled by the darkness of her skin from exposure to the sun. She is concerned about her appearance because she wants to look her very best and be pleasing to Solomon. She compares her appearance to **the tents of Kedar**. The reference to **Kedar** is to the desert area of eastern Syria and present day Jordan. The Kedarites were a nomadic Arabic people that trace back to the second son of Ishmael (Genesis 24:13) and lived in tents (see Jeremiah 49:28-29) made from animal skins (some scholars indicate black goats), which like her present beauty is a darkened color.

She likewise compares her complexion to **the curtains of Solomon**, which no doubt were made of the finest fabrics and thus were beautiful, but like her, they were dark in color. Those **curtains were** possibly purple, a color associated with wealth and royalty, but also may have been black.

Although Shulamite laments her failure to tend her **own vineyard**, she does not obsess on it but moves on to happier thoughts, namely about her lover, who she longs to be with. Again, it is critical to keep in mind the context. Shulamite is recalling a period in her life when she had fallen in love and was to be married, but until the wedding she and her lover are in some sense separated. No doubt they could see each other, but until the wedding there were boundaries in their relationship. Shulamite longs for the wedding and the consummation of their marriage when the boundaries will be removed. But until that time, in poetic terms, the Song will again and again focus on their separation and the boundaries in their relationship. And if we focus too hard on trying to take every line of the Song in a rigidly literal way so that we can build a linear story (what we may term the "Heartbreak Hotel" folly), we miss the literary purpose in what we read. Accordingly, when Shulamite asks the question, **tell me, O thou whom my soul loveth, where thou feedest** your flock, **where thou makest thy flock to rest at noon**, what is introduced in physical terms (his absence from her) is her feeling of separation from him while the boundaries remain in place.

From this verse, many expositors understand that Shulamite's lover is a shepherd. It is for this reason that many take it that there are two lovers in the Song, a young shepherd and Solomon. The better view is that her only lover is Solomon, again within the poetic use of his name and person within the Song. Some believe the shepherd is the wealthy Solomon, but that Shulamite is at this point unaware of his true identity and thinks he is a mere shepherd. But again we must keep in mind that we are reading a song that seeks to express Shulamite's emotions and feelings in poetic terms and imagery, and here, her feelings of separation and her longing to be with her lover are expressed with the imagery of him being a shepherd camped out of town whom she longs to find; later in the Song, her lover will be pictured as royalty in the person of Solomon. According to 1 Kings 10:23: "So king Solomon exceeded all the kings of the earth for riches and for wisdom." Thus, Solomon likely owned flocks of sheep, but it is improbable that he personally tended to his flocks. These difficulties need not necessarily be resolved, but in my view the shepherd imagery is simply used because within her culture the imagery would be widely understood. Shepherds led their flocks outside the cities and had to stay with the flocks, thus providing the very picture of unavailability and separation. Shulamite's separation from and inability to find her lover will be a recurring theme, albeit with different imagery to paint the picture of separation.

Shulamite asks another question, which like the first, is addressed to her absent lover, and therefore only the chorus may respond. She asks, **for why should I be as one that turneth aside by the flocks of thy companions?** She longs to know where he is at so that she need not wander about looking for him as if she were lost. The reality is that without knowing where he is, she has little chance of finding him. It makes little sense to think that, if

Shulamite and the shepherd are very much in love, she would have no idea where he pastures his sheep. Again, the primary purpose of this imagery is to convey her emotions as she longs to be with him as his wife, but it is not time yet and so there remain boundaries of separation between them during the courtship period. Those insurmountable boundaries are likened to her not knowing where her lover is, and this separation will remain until the day of the wedding.

> DAUGHTERS
>
> <u>8</u> If thou know not,
> O thou fairest among women,
> go thy way forth by the footsteps of the flock,
> and feed thy kids beside the shepherds' tents.

Here in verse 8, many expositors and modern translations take the speaker to be Shulamite's lover, but there are difficulties with that view. First, Shulamite is expressly addressing the "daughters of Jerusalem" as she begins in verse 5. Although her question in verse 7 is ostensibly addressed to "thou whom my soul loveth," her lover is not present or else she would not be asking the question. Only the chorus can answer her and provide a transition to the lover's words that begin in verse 9. Second, the phrase **thou fairest among women** occurs only here in verse 8 and in verses 5:9 and 6:1, and the latter two instances are plainly the "daughters" or chorus speaking to her. It therefore makes sense from the standpoint of consistency and the immediate context that the chorus is also addressing Shulamite here as **thou fairest among women**. Third, if this is the response of her lover, why does he not simply answer the question as to his location or come to her? Instead, the response is advice and not a direct answer to her question.

The daughters praise her as **thou fairest among women** in response to her self-conscious concerns about her skin complexion, and then advise her about how to find her lover, namely to **go thy way forth by the footsteps of the flock**. In other words, the daughters tell Shulamite to follow the footprints from his flock and track down her lover. Further, they advise her to **feed thy kids** (little lambs) **beside the shepherds' tents**. By this means, she will not be conspicuous as she searches for him since she would have her own sheep as an apparent excuse for being there. Their advice suggests that by doing so, he will find her when the time is appropriate. Notice that the text does not indicate that Shulamite actually tracked **the footsteps of the flock**, for that is not the purpose of the chorus here. Rather, the purpose is two-fold. First, the chorus extols Shulamite as **thou fairest among women**, providing a transition between her self-assessment of her physical appearance and her lover's admiration in verses 9 through 11. Second, the chorus' advice acknowledges her deep longing to be with her lover and that the appropriate time for their physical union is near but not yet by painting the picture of her tracking his flock's footsteps yet still waiting for him to find her.

SOLOMON

9 I have compared thee, O my love,

to a company of horses in Pharaoh's chariots.

10 Thy cheeks are comely with rows *of jewels*,

thy neck with chains *of gold*.

11 We will make thee borders of gold

with studs of silver.

Here, Shulamite's lover speaks for the first time and, in contrast to her reservations about her physical appearance, he greatly admires her beauty. Indeed, Solomon **compared** Shulamite **(O my love), to a company of horses in Pharaoh's chariots.** Throughout the Song, as the two lovers admire one another, the imagery they employ, though magnificent, is a creature of its time and culture. One thing the Song is not is a "how to" for speaking romantically to your significant other (i.e., husbands are ill-advised to compare their wife to a horse today and do so at their own peril), but the principle of verbalizing admiration for their attributes in appropriate modern language is clear. The **Pharaoh's** horses were stallions dressed in decorative and even jeweled coverings, which makes sense of the focus in verses 10 and 11 on jewelry. Her lover remarks that her **cheeks are comely** or beautiful **with rows of jewels** and that her **neck** is beautiful **with chains of gold.** He further states that **we will make thee borders** or ornaments (jewelry) **of gold with studs of silver.** Additional jewelry to adorn her beauty will be provided to her. Later in the Song, Shulamite's lover will describe her beauty unclothed and in significantly more detail. Here, his admiration is strong but the description is based on her physical beauty while fully clothed and, accordingly, is more limited.

In view of the description here of Shulamite, arrayed like the **horses of Pharaoh's chariots** and wearing fine jewelry, this portion of the Song likely is a reflection on the wedding day. Her lover sees her and like any bride arrayed for the big day, Shulamite is glowing. Her response that follows gives credence to the fact that they are now together, likely at the wedding feast.

SHULAMITE

12 While the king *sitteth* at his table,

my spikenard sendeth forth the smell thereof.

13 A bundle of myrrh *is* my wellbeloved unto me;

he shall lie all night betwixt my breasts.

14 My beloved *is* unto me *as* a cluster of camphire

in the vineyards of Engedi.

Shulamite responds to her lover's admiration, saying that **while the king sitteth at his table,** her **spikenard sendeth forth the smell thereof.** The reference here is to a banqueting table, suggesting again that the setting is the wedding feast on the day of their wedding. Shulamite is obviously present and perhaps also seated at **his table.** Note here that her lover is referred to as **the king,** which will occur again in 3:9, 3:11 and 7:5; this supports the view that her lover is Solomon, although again we must emphasize that as a song it need not necessarily recount actual history nor do the references to **the king** or Solomon need to necessarily indicate a recording of historical events since the poet (here Solomon) is free to use a historical figure, even himself, for effect (i.e., he could be her personal Solomon just as a man today may refer to his wife or fiancé as his princess or queen without it needing to be literal) as was common in ancient literature. As indicated before, resolving this issue is unimportant to grasping the overall message of the Song.

Nard or **spikenard** was an aromatic oil from a plant used as perfume, and while she cannot yet physically reach out to him, the aroma is intended to reach her lover and invite him to her. The consummation of the marriage will soon occur, and indeed Shulamite comments that her **wellbeloved** is a **bundle of myrrh...unto** her. The term **myrrh** refers to an aromatic gum (or resin) from the bark of a tree, which like **spikenard** was expensive and imported into Israel. In solid form it was placed in a pouch and worn close to the body, and it is this picture she implies when she says that her lover is a **bundle of myrrh...unto** her. In other words, he is soon to be physically close to her as they consummate the marriage, and in fact, like a pouch of **myrrh** hanging on a necklace between the breasts, **he shall lie all night betwixt** her **breasts**. Similarly, her **beloved is unto** her **as a cluster of camphire** or henna blossoms **in the vineyards of Engedi**. Again the imagery relies on scent to convey sensuality. **Camphire** is an archaic term for henna, a shrub whose blossoms are aromatic and used to make perfume, among other products. **Engedi** is an oasis on the southwestern shore of the Dead Sea, a picture of green in the middle of a desert that supported lush vegetation such as the **camphire**. Her Solomon is a fragrant oasis that she may soon enter and enjoy as the marriage is consummated.

## Closing

A child waits for Christmas with great anticipation, counting down the days. The child is unsure of what is in those boxes under the tree, but confident that it is all good. The child can hardly fall asleep the night before because of the anticipation, and then springs out of bed an hour early to open gifts. But if the child sneaks a peak or somehow figures out a week before Christmas what the gifts are, Christmas morning will still come and gifts will be opened, but the experience loses something.

Truly, anticipation is a powerful elixir, and a healthy and normal emotion before big events, like Christmas morning in the life of a child, and the wedding night in the life of a young couple. In the life of an engaged couple, anticipation during courtship is to be enjoyed but managed.

## Application Points

- **MAIN PRINCIPLE:** With mutually recognized boundaries in place, physical desire and anticipation before a marriage is consummated is normal and healthy.

- It is healthy to have a balanced view of one's physical features, and within that context to seek to look our best for our mate.

- We should learn to appreciate and praise our spouse's physical features.

## Discussion Questions

1. Assuming the Song is about physical romance within marriage, what is its importance to the overall theology of the Bible? Necessary, critical, unnecessary, helpful, obsolete, obscene, etc.?

2. From Shulamite's description, what do we know about Solomon that makes him exceptional?

3. Do we know from the text whether Shulamite is beautiful by the standards of her day, or instead, beautiful in Solomon's eyes? Does it matter?

4. Should a person attempt to be physically pleasing to their spouse in how they look, dress, groom, hygiene, etc.? Why?

5. When you think of what your concept of what life as a woman was like in the ancient world, is what we learn of Shulamite in the 1:1-14 consistent with that concept?

6. God created marriage "in the beginning." Why did God create sex? What are the implications of sex being by God's design for humanity?

# Chapter 2

# The Right Person and Right Time

A common teaching on marriage is that God has picked "the one" but not disclosed his or her identity to us and so it is up to us to seek and find "the one" God selected. Even in secular teaching, we hear about "finding your soul mate." Of course, the secular world also talks of "falling in love" like a healthy relationship is a hole in the ground. The truth is far from it. What the Bible teaches is that we make a commitment in marriage and by God's hand the two become one. Jesus remarked that "what therefore God hath joined together...." An enduring and fulfilling marriage happens neither by accident nor magic, but is the product of mutual commitment. The great Puritan poet Anne Bradstreet understood love within marriage, as expressed in her beautiful poem, "To my Dear and loving Husband":

> If ever two were one, then surely we.
> If ever man were lov'd by wife, then thee;
> If ever wife was happy in a man,

Compare with me ye women if you can.
I prize thy love more than whole Mines of gold,
Or all the riches that the East doth hold.
My love is such that Rivers cannot quench,
Nor ought but love from thee, give recompence.
Thy love is such I can no way repay,
The heavens reward thee manifold I pray.
Then while we live, in love lets so persever,
That when we live no more, we may live ever.

Such a love as she had for her husband, and as Shulamite had for Solomon, was not built on a foundation of physical pleasures. Rather, the physical pleasures flowed out of their love and commitment. The Song teaches us that sexual pleasure is reserved for the right person at the right time. From passages in the Song and elsewhere in the Bible, the right person has to do with selecting a spouse with character and a desire to grow in the Lord to whom one makes a permanent commitment. The passage under consideration in this chapter presents the core wisdom of the Song, namely that sex is reserved exclusively for the right person at the right time, and the right time is within the marriage context and not before. The Song views the sexual pleasures within marriage as a natural outflow of a strong committed relationship that cannot be achieved outside of the marriage covenant.

## Scripture And Comments

In Song 1:1-14, we saw that Shulamite expressed anticipation of her wedding night and the consummation of the marriage as she longed to be with Solomon and enter the next phase of her life, i.e., marriage. But until the wedding, there are boundaries established in the relationship that are reflected by the imagery of Solomon as a shepherd separated from Shulamite in some unknown location. Both Song 1:1-14 and the passage under consideration in this chapter, Song 1:14-2:7, are part of Shulamite's reflection on her wedding day just prior to the consummation of the marriage. In Song 1:14-2:7, Shulamite will express that it is now the season for lovemaking, each will praise the other as singularly above and superior to their peers, Shulamite will express her great anticipation of making love to Solomon, and she will charge the daughters of Jerusalem with the core wisdom teaching of the book, namely that sexual pleasures are reserved for the right person at the right time.

SOLOMON

Song 1:15 Behold, thou *art* fair, my love;

behold, thou *art* fair;

thou *hast* doves' eyes.

Shulamite's lover responds to her, **thou art fair** or beautiful, **my love** or **my** darling. So arrested with her beauty, Solomon again exclaims, **behold, thou art fair**. Before he focused on her apparel and jewelry, but now on her **eyes**, described as **doves' eyes**. We must understand that she is likely arrayed in a long robe that covers nearly all of her body except her **eyes**, making them a particularly prominent feature of what he can see. That is why his description before and now is necessarily limited. The full significance of the phrase **doves' eyes** is widely debated, although obviously a complement of her strikingly beautiful eyes. This imagery will be used again in the Song and the reader is referred to the notes on Song 5:12.

SHULAMITE

<u>16</u> Behold, thou *art* fair, my beloved,

yea, pleasant:

also our bed *is* green.

<u>17</u> The beams of our house *are* cedar,

*and* our rafters of fir.

Shulamite responds in kind to Solomon's admiration, **behold thou art fair, my beloved, yea pleasant** or delightful. She continues with the comment, **also our bed is green.** One way to take these verses is that the two lovers are laying on the grass talking and looking up at the trees, thus likening a natural setting to their wedding bed. Because earlier verses indicated that Shulamite is most likely arrayed for her wedding and her king is at the banqueting table, the comments she makes here are better understood as figurative in nature, which also best fits the repeated figurative use later in the Song of gardens, vineyards, plants and trees with sexual overtones. As she eagerly anticipates the consummation of their marriage, Shulamite's words that **our bed is green** is a statement that their marriage bed is ready, that is, that they have reached the appropriate time to consummate the marriage. The **bed is green** because it is the Spring season when the flora blooms and grows to a lush state (in contrast to the Fall and Winter). Just as it is the right time for the foliage to abound, it is the right time for their sexual union—the waiting is over. It is helpful to keep in mind that in Jewish wedding traditions, the man would prepare the bedroom for his bride, and here the statements that **the beams of our house are cedar, and our rafters of fir**, suggests both that the marital bedroom is ready and that it is lavish. Again, the bed and the bedroom being ready mean that the time is now at hand when they can make love as husband and wife.

SHULAMITE

<u>Song 2:1</u> I *am* the rose of Sharon,

*and* the lily of the valleys.

The scene now transitions from the wedding feast to the bedroom and then Shulamite will speak wisdom to the daughters of Jerusalem. The transition begins as she refers to herself as **the rose of Sharon, and the lily of the valleys**. The area of **Sharon** is the coastal plains south of Mount Carmel (meaning God's vineyard) in northern Israel. She refers to herself as a common flower found in **Sharon** or a common **lily** found in **the valleys**. As in chapter 1, Shulamite's self-assessment of her physical appearance reflects that she does not see herself as flawlessly beautiful, but her lover will respond and explain that she is, in his eyes, the very best with no equal among her peers. I do note here that people have often taken these descriptions (**rose of Sharon** and **lily of the valleys**) to refer to Jesus. Things that "sound good" or "preach" (or sing) well are often untrue; here in 2:1, it is the female character speaking, not the male, and so there is no basis for understanding "rose of Sharon" or "lily of the valleys" as allegorical symbols for Jesus.

SOLOMON

<u>2</u> As the lily among thorns,

so *is* my love among the daughters.

Shulamite's lover is quick to respond to her self-evaluation as average or common by articulating her superiority over other women. Rather than being a common **lily** among many others—in other words, **among the daughters**—his **love** Shulamite is a **lily among thorns** by comparison.    This is no criticism of the **daughters**, but simply a statement of Shulamite's superiority in Solomon's eyes.  She is to her lover quite singular and extraordinary, and he is ever ready to verbalize his feelings in this regard.

> SHULAMITE
>
> 3 As the apple tree among the trees of the wood,
>
> so *is* my beloved among the sons.
>
> I sat down under his shadow with great delight,
>
> and his fruit *was* sweet to my taste.
>
> 4 He brought me to the banqueting house,
>
> and his banner over me *was* love.
>
> 5 Stay me with flagons,
>
> comfort me with apples:
>
> for I *am* sick of love.
>
> 6 His left hand *is* under my head,
>
> and his right hand doth embrace me.
>
> 7 I charge you, O ye daughters of Jerusalem,
>
> by the roes, and by the hinds of the field,
>
> that ye stir not up, nor awake *my* love,
>
> till he please.

Now Shulamite returns the praise to her lover, and just as he considered her a "lily among thorns," she considers her **beloved... as the apple tree among the trees of the wood** or forest.  Just as Shulamite is in Solomon's eyes far better than any of the other daughters of Jerusalem, so is he elevated in her eyes **among the sons**.  Of course, among ordinary trees, the **apple tree** stands out because it produces nourishing and tasteful fruit; and also in this context, because the **apple tree** was not native to Israel but had to be imported, such a **tree** would always stand out among other trees. Shulamite will again refer to the **apple tree** in 8:5, though there she will not call her lover an **apple tree**. In both instances, the symbolism of the **apple tree** is sexually charged, and indeed here, Shulamite explains that she takes **great delight** in sitting **down under his shadow**. Further, **his fruit was** (or is) **sweet to** her **taste**. As she begins reminiscing in verse 4 about their coming together on the wedding night, Shulamite makes a generalized statement, in poetic terms, of enjoying him physically. A note of caution here—we need to read the Song as poetry and not try to discern from **his fruit was** (or is) **sweet to my taste** the details of precisely what transpires and in what sequence when they make love. The point is not to understand the Song in terms of "you can do this in bed with your spouse" but "you cannot do this." Rather, the Song expresses their lovemaking qualitatively and poetically to extol its beauty. As the author of Hebrews commented: "Marriage is honourable in all, and the bed undefiled...." (Hebrews 13:4) So long as their lovemaking is within the context of marriage and mutually consented, there is liberty of discovery.

In verse 4, Shulamite begins describing some of the wedding details as the moment of the consummation of their marriage is near at hand. She explains that **he brought me to the banqueting house** or **banqueting** hall. In other words, she remembers their wedding day while they were at the wedding feast, although in her description it is as if only the two of them were present.

At the feast, her lover's **banner** or flag **over** her **was love**. Here, the term **love** is the Hebrew *ahavah* and according to Strong's means affection. In other words, she has his complete attention and the **banner** of affection **over** her is his affectionately looking at her. Shulamite longs to be able to move from the public **banqueting house** to the privacy of the marriage bedroom and desires that her lover would **stay** or sustain her **with flagons** or raisin cakes in the meantime, considered an aphrodisiac in the ancient world, and no doubt preparatory to their lovemaking. Similarly, she wants him to **comfort** her **with apples**. Notwithstanding the reference in verse 3 to enjoying **his fruit** (apples), at the moment she was at the wedding feast she had not yet made love to him, but she is ready. Indeed, she is **sick of** or faint with **love** or affection. In other words, the anticipation of the moment when she can make love to Solomon is overwhelming to her, and because of this figurative faintness, she needs to be fed or satisfied with **flagons** and **apples** until she is finally able make love to him.

As the Song edges closer to the actual consummation of the wedding, her lover's **left hand is under** her **head, and his right hand doth embrace me**. This suggests that they are no longer in the banqueting room, but laying down in the bedroom embracing as the moment is finally at hand. The same expression will appear again in 8:3 in the context of Shulamite's expressed desire to make love to Solomon. Having finally moved to this moment, Shulamite speaks to the chorus: **I charge you, O ye daughters of Jerusalem**. We must remember that the Song, like Proverbs and Ecclesiastes, is wisdom literature. And while there are a number of applications to be made, the central wisdom is addressed to the young women of marriageable age, similar to how much of the wisdom in the book of Proverbs is addressed by a father to a son.

This central piece of wisdom is the theme of the book and is repeated as wisdom to the chorus in Song 3:5 and 8:4. She adjures these maidens **by the roes** or gazelles, **and by the hinds** (young does) **of the field** or open country. The question is why **charge** them with the witness of these animals? These graceful creatures symbolize love and sexuality as it should be experienced and enjoyed. (See Song 2:9, 17, 8:14; Proverbs 5:19) So important is this wisdom that Shulamite has for the maidens that, in the form of an oath, she affirms the veracity of her wisdom by appealing to the **roes** and **hinds** as witnesses to what she has to say. This is similar to statements like "I call heaven and earth to witness against you this day..." (Deuteronomy 4:26) and "Hear, O heavens, and give ear, O earth...." (Isaiah 1:2) In a song where physical love within marriage is highly exalted, Shulamite appeals to physical love as her witness, charging the maidens not to **stir...up, nor awake *my* love, till he please**. Note that the word *my* is in italics in the KJV because it does not appear in the text. What she is saying to the maidens is not to **awake** or stir up physical passions until the appropriate time. The central wisdom of the Song is that sexual love is a glorious experience of tremendous pleasure and value by God's design, but must be experienced with the right person at the right time. To stir passions prematurely will diminish the experience and the maidens are admonished to wait.

Our modern culture derides such wisdom as old-fashioned, unrealistic, and even unhealthy. There is not space enough here to address this issue fully, but some comments are in order. First of all, God's wisdom on this issue cannot be questioned. The Song candidly concedes that before the wedding night Shulamite desired to make love to her beloved. But like all restrictions in the Bible, this one is for our benefit and our best interest. God never hides His best from us. God says (through both lovers) that the experience—not only initially but in the long run of the marriage as later verses will make clear—will be the very best for those who, like Shulamite and Solomon, do not prematurely surrender to physical passions but instead await the right person and the right time. The reality is that premature sexual relationships affect future relationships. The long-term commitment necessary to a healthy marriage becomes increasingly difficult in each subsequent sexual relationship, and notably, the divorce rate increases exponentially with each subsequent marriage. It should also be noted that if a person is coerced to comply with physical advances, there will often be long-term emotional effects even within a marriage to the one who coerced sex prematurely. Someone will surely ask the question, why does it matter if we are going to get married anyway? It matters because God says that whatever you think you are going to experience now would have been better had you waited, and as the One who created marriage to begin with, God knows best. God's intent is that the sexual pleasures flow from the foundation of a healthy marriage relationship rather than a couple attempting to use physical pleasures as the foundation for a subsequent marriage relationship.

As Christians, we need to learn to take God at His Word regardless of whether we think we know better. "Trust in the LORD with all thine heart; and lean not unto thine own understanding." (Proverbs 3:5) This matters because if the relationship sours, those sexual experiences become baggage carried into the next relationship that may devalue the sexual experience there or inhibit its full enjoyment. In light of all of this, during the courtship phase of the relationship, there should be mutually agreed and discussed boundaries that allow the relationship to develop and flourish on the basis of commitment, learning, trusting and growing together as best friends. What all too often occurs is that premature sex creates a sort of "Hollywood phase" in which the physical pleasures are the primary foundation of the relationship and give the illusion of substance, but when the "Hollywood phase" is over, the couple finds that the relationship lacks the foundational elements (e.g., commitment, friendship, trust, non-physical intimacy) necessary for an enduring marriage.

## Closing

When we think of the world's greatest love stories, we think of couples like Romeo and Juliet, Mark Antony and Cleopatra, Pyramus and Thisbe, John Smith and Pocahontas, and Salim and Anarkali. It seems that in every great love story, the lovers find in one another a completion to their world. The world is their beloved and no one else. The reality is that we know little of Solomon's and Shulamite's physical appearance. But what we do know is that each was in the other's eyes wholly unique, uncommon, and in a league of their own. All others are just background noise in the world sculpted by their love and affection. Shulamite is a lily among thorns, and Solomon an apple tree among the ordinary trees of the forest. It matters not what the world sees in either of them, physically or otherwise, but only what they see through their eyes and hearts in one another. But more than just seeing and enjoying these qualities in one another, they are great communicators and that skill sets them apart from most couples. Neither of them is perfect, yet each measures the other by their positive qualities. Each builds up and encourages the other, verbalizing their specialness. Kind and edifying words expressing their mutual love and affection paint their world and give substance to their passionate speech, elevating it above lust to the realm of a sustaining delight in one another even before the marriage is consummated. The tremendous value of what they have is the direct result of Shulamite and Solomon delaying physical romance for the right person at the right time. Rather than trying to build a marriage relationship on hormones, a foundation of affection, friendship, love and commitment is established before the marriage, which can then be expressed physically at the right time and in that context their sexual experience will itself be enhanced.

## Application Points

- **MAIN PRINCIPLE:** Sexual pleasure is to be reserved for the right person only in the context of marriage and not before.

- The relationship prior to marriage (the courtship phase) should be developed with mutually agreed boundaries in place.

- Identify the positive qualities in your spouse (significant other) and verbalize those qualities.

## Discussion Questions

1. Is it important to you to hear your spouse articulate how you are special to him/her?

2. What can you do to make your marriage a safe place for honest and open communications?

3. If compliments are only offered in the context of lovemaking, what signal does that send?

4. What is the culture's view of waiting until marriage to engage in sex? Why do you think that is the case?

5. Is the Bible just "old fashioned" in what it says about sex?

6. Are there negative consequences to having other lovers before you get married? If so, what are they?

7. Are there negative consequences for two Christians who are engaged having sex before they get married? If so, what are they?

8. What can we give to our spouse that we have given to no one else?

# Chapter 3

# The Courtship

In the ancient world, walls were critical to the defense of a city. So important were walls that much of the book of Nehemiah centers on the rebuilding of the wall of Jerusalem so that it can be defended. Before Nehemiah oversaw the rebuilding of the wall, God promised through the prophet Zechariah to be a "wall of fire" about the city. In the book of Joshua, the key to Israel taking Jericho was God's supernatural destruction of the city's tremendous walls. When you look at what is left of the castles built in the last thousand years, unless they are just single towers, there invariably are defensive walls surrounding the castles. Those walls were not in place to trap the citizens within and withhold from them the benefits that might be available outside the walls. Instead, the walls were there to protect the inhabitants.

Walled cities and castles are a useful analogy for the Word of God. In the Garden, God made available to Adam and Eve every tree but one, and it is in our human nature to take for granted the thousands of trees at our disposal and focus on the one that is off limits. But like defensive walls, God's restrictions in the Bible are for our benefit and protection, not to withhold His best from us. Even if we cannot fully comprehend the adverse consequences of disobedience to God's Word and ignoring God's wisdom, the fact remains that God places walls in our lives for our good. It should come as no surprise to us that in the realm of relationships and sexuality, God places boundaries. Far too many couples today ignore those boundaries or reason that the boundaries do not apply to them. But in the Song, Solomon and Shulamite mutually recognized the boundaries and the core wisdom of the Song is that the boundaries were in their best interest and they benefited tremendously by waiting until they were married to engage in sex. But the Song does not ignore the reality of their anticipation and how the boundaries precipitated strong feelings of separation as they awaited the wedding day. Yet in the final analysis, the Song recognizes these natural feelings but still urges us not to cross the boundaries until the proper time when God removes them. The issue for us is not whether God placed boundaries for our good, but whether we will trust His wisdom in this area of our lives and enjoy the blessings of a proper courtship that issues from the hand of God rather than being preoccupied with the blessing God asks us to wait for.

## Scripture And Comments

In Song 1:15-2:7, we found that Solomon brought Shulamite to the banqueting hall for the wedding. At last, the wait for the consummation of their marriage would shortly be over. Expressing her emotions at that moment, Shulamite related that she is "sick of love" or lovesick. She was figuratively faint with anticipation and called upon Solomon to sustain her with raisin cakes and apples. But even in the midst of expressing her strong desire to be with Solomon, Shulamite charged the daughters of Jerusalem concerning the wisdom of waiting for the proper time for lovemaking. We will see in the passage under consideration in this chapter that the Song is not strictly chronological, and in particular, Shulamite will now reflect back on her courtship with Solomon and the strong feelings of separation she experienced in the long wait for their wedding day. We will also see that after recognizing these powerful emotions and the strong desire to be with Solomon, Shulamite again reiterated her wisdom about honoring the boundaries by reserving sexual pleasures for marriage.

SHULAMITE

Song 2:8 The voice of my beloved!

behold, he cometh leaping upon the mountains,

skipping upon the hills.

9 My beloved is like a roe

or a young hart:

behold, he standeth behind our wall,

he looketh forth at the windows,

shewing himself through the lattice.

10 My beloved spake, and said unto me,

Having charged the chorus to wait for the right person and the right time before engaging in sexual love, Shulamite returns in her mind to their courtship days when she experienced anticipation, desire, and feelings of separation. I would suggest that this sequence (2:8-2:17) is either a daydream (imaginative musing while Shulamite is awake) or possibly a dream sequence like the next (3:1-4). This is suggested by the surreal nature of what transpires. Shulamite hears **the voice of** her **beloved** calling her from a great distance as he hurries to her. As if speaking still to the chorus, she says **behold** or look there at Solomon, **he cometh leaping upon the mountains, skipping upon the hills.** Her lover is the picture of virility as he skips the tops of mountains to get to her, all of which describes a scene more like a dream than reality. Her physically impressive **beloved is like a roe** (gazelle) **or a young hart** (stag). Yet when he arrives to meet her, **he standeth behind our wall, he looketh forth at the windows, shewing himself through the lattice**. The wall separates them, but as the moment of the wedding and consummation approaches, he calls her to himself. It is helpful to keep in mind that, consistent with Jewish wedding practices, during the courtship and betrothal period Shulamite would await the day when, unannounced, her beloved would come to her to take her away with him to the wedding. Thus, it is natural that Shulamite would dream or daydream about Solomon's heroic arrival to escort here away, especially as she knew from the passage of time that the day was approaching.

SOLOMON

Rise up, my love,

my fair one, and come away.

11 For, lo, the winter is past,

the rain is over *and* gone;

12 The flowers appear on the earth;

the time of the singing *of birds* is come,

and the voice of the turtle is heard in our land;

13 The fig tree putteth forth her green figs,

and the vines *with* the tender grape give a *good* smell.

Arise, my love,

my fair one, and come away.

14 O my dove, *that art* in the clefts of the rock,

in the secret *places* of the stairs,

let me see thy countenance,

let me hear thy voice;

for sweet *is* thy voice,

and thy countenance *is* comely.

Through the lattice Solomon beckons Shulamite, **rise up, my love, my fair** or beautiful **one, and come away**. Her lover will use the imagery of the change of seasons to denote that it is now the time or season for lovemaking. Again, we must keep in mind the central wisdom of the book—physical romance is designed for the right person at the right time. No doubt, she has found the right person and now it is the time or season that is at issue. The season for courtship is past and the season for marriage and lovemaking has arrived. In fact, **winter is past, the rain is over and gone, the flowers appear on the earth, the time of the singing of birds is come, and the voice of the turtle** dove **is heard in our land**. In other words, it is springtime now when **flowers** bloom and **birds** sing. It is the time when **the fig tree putteth forth her green figs, and the vines with tender grape give a good smell**. Throughout the Song, as here, imagery of lush gardens, aromatic fragrances, and ripe fruit are used to convey physical desire and sexuality and even the physical body, and the point here is that while those things were not ready before, they are ready (or ripe) now for enjoyment. And since the season is now appropriate, he calls upon Shulamite to **arise...and come away**. She is his **love** and his **fair** or beautiful **one**. Of course, what is in view is not a literal change of seasons nor a literal journey that he is calling her to. The imagery conveys that the courtship phase is past and it is now the season for marriage and lovemaking, and for that reason, Shulamite's lover invites her to go away with him.

Yet, she is still Solomon's **dove...in the clefts of the rock**. As a bird hidden away **in the clefts of the rock** she is physically inaccessible, just as she is on the other side of the wall in the prior verses. From both of their perspectives, prior to their wedding there are boundaries (symbolized by the inaccessibility) that cannot be crossed. She is **in the secret** or hiding **places of the stairs** or crevices within the mountain, beyond his reach. He requests the opportunity to **see** her **countenance** (her face), which is **comely or beautiful**, and **hear** her **voice** again, which is **sweet**. He longs for the wall to come down and the separation to end so that they can marry and he can make love to Shulamite.

SHULAMITE

15 Take us the foxes,

the little foxes, that spoil the vines:

for our vines *have* tender grapes.

16 My beloved *is* mine, and I *am* his:

he feedeth among the lilies.

17 Until the day break,

and the shadows flee away,

> turn, my beloved, and be thou like a roe
>
> or a young hart upon the mountains of Bether.

Shulamite acknowledges the figurative change of seasons from Fall to Spring when she honors Solomon's request to hear her voice and says, **take us the foxes, the little foxes, that spoil the vines, for our vines have tender grapes**. Often this verse is used to teach that within a marriage, small problems (small foxes) should be addressed before they become large problems (large foxes), and surely that is good wisdom, but that is not what this verse is saying nor does any of the preceding or succeeding context support that view. At this point in her reminiscing they are not even married yet, and her words are in direct response to Solomon's longing to hear her voice after a long period of separation, to which a discussion about addressing their relationship problems would be wholly out of accord. Rather, Shulamite agrees with her lover that spring is here by building on the imagery he began. Solomon noted that "the vines *with* the tender grape give a *good* smell," to which she agrees, so much so that the grapes have even attracted the **little** or young **foxes**. Noting the presence of the **little foxes** is no different than her lover noting the presence of the birds singing. Spring is in the air and the season for marriage and lovemaking has finally come, for winter (the courtship time with its boundaries and separation) is past.

Shulamite exclaims that **my beloved is mine, and I am his: he feedeth** or grazes **among the lilies**, which she will repeat in 6:3. Some have taken the words **he feedeth among the lilies** to refer to lovemaking, but the line seems to be in parallel to the previous line, thus indicating the quality of their relationship, and in particular that he is wholly satisfied (sustained as he feeds) in his relationship to her because of their mutual commitment to one another. Despite the boundaries of courtship, the relationship is wholly satisfying. This view makes better sense of the next verse, where she calls upon her lover **until the day break, and the shadows flee away**, in other words until morning, to make love to her. She says to **turn** from where you are feeding, **my beloved, and be thou like a roe or a young hart** climbing **upon the mountains of Bether**. The reference to **mountains of Bether** is not to a place, but means divided **mountains,** which is imagery for her breasts. Just as these animals (**a roe or a young hart**) would climb the **mountains**, so she calls upon her lover to climb her breasts, i.e., to make love to her. The marriage is not consummated at this point; rather, Shulamite recognized that the season has finally arrived and called upon her Solomon, while he grazed **among the lilies** to come to her, which is a fitting response to his invitation in 2:10 to come away with him.

SHULAMITE

<u>Song 3:1</u> By night on my bed
I sought him whom my soul loveth:
I sought him, but I found him not.
<u>2</u> I will rise now, and go about the city
in the streets, and in the broad ways
I will seek him whom my soul loveth:
I sought him, but I found him not.
3 The watchmen that go about the city found me:
*to whom I said*, Saw ye him whom my soul loveth?
4 *It was* but a little that I passed from them,
but I found him whom my soul loveth:

I held him, and would not let him go,
until I had brought him into my mother's house,
and into the chamber of her that conceived me.
5 I charge you, O ye daughters of Jerusalem,
by the roes, and by the hinds of the field,
that ye stir not up, nor awake *my* love,
till he please.

Shulamite now returns to expressing her feelings of separation and anticipation as she looked forward to the wedding and the consummation of their marriage. These, of course, are quite normal emotions. Here, and again in 5:2-7, Shulamite dreams. And in dreams, what occurs seems rational during the dream and often irrational upon waking up. What we see in the dream is surreal, and thus as we attempt to interpret the dream passages, we need to be mindful that we are reading poetry in the context of a dream where the events need not be rational. Rather, the purpose of the dream is to convey her deepest emotions. As she recounts the dream, **by night on my bed I sought him** in a dream **whom my soul loveth: I sought him, but I found him not**. We again find Shulamite feeling separated, and indeed abandoned, by her lover, just as in 1:7 where he was pictured as a shepherd outside the city in some unknown location feeding his flock. Here, Shulamite is unaware of Solomon's location, but he is presumably within the city. And so she determines to **rise now, and go about the city in the streets and in the broad ways** to **seek him whom my soul loveth**. Thus, within the dream, she walks about the city seeking her lover, but she **found him not**. What she did find was the **watchmen** or guards **that go about the city** (technically, they **found** her). She asked them, **Saw ye him whom my soul loveth?** No response is given; the guards are authority figures that represent boundaries between her and her lover, just as elsewhere she is separated from him by geography (1:7) and a locked door (5:2).

Next, after **a little** while, Shulamite **passed from** the guards and **found him whom my soul loveth**. So pleased to find her Solomon and fearful of losing him, she **held him, and would not let go, until** she **brought him into** her **mother's house, and into the chamber of her that conceived me**. Again, all of this is poetic and within a dream. Shulamite falls asleep thinking ahead to their wedding day and longing to be together with her lover, then dreams about him being lost in the city and her searching for him in the night, none of which is rational but it paints the picture both of their separation (the boundaries of not yet being married) and her longing to be together with him as husband and wife. No wonder, then, that when she finds him, she will **not let go**. In the dream, she will not let him go until she could sequester him to her **mother's house**. While the significance of this imagery is uncertain, Shulamite plainly finds significance in the notion of making love to him in the very bedroom where she was conceived. Likewise, in chapter 8, Shulamite will speak of making love to him where he was conceived. Note additional parallels in the two passages, although the motifs in chapter 8 are presented in a different order (compare 3:4 to second half of 8:5, 3:5 to 8:4, 3:6 to first half of 8:5). There appears to be great significance to a sort of cycle of life being completed.

Having again stressed her longing to make love to her beloved, Shulamite gives her **charge** to the **daughters of Jerusalem**, in identical terms as she did in 2:7, and the reader should refer to the notes there. In short, Shulamite reiterates her central wisdom for the maidens, namely that they should not awaken sexual passions prematurely, but instead wait for the right person and the right time to do so. As the Song unfolds, the beautiful imagery describing Shulamite's physical union with her husband exalts the value of the sexual relationship within the confines of marriage that is otherwise unattainable, and possibly lost altogether, if the maidens do not heed her advice.


## Closing

Who has not experienced watching the clock waiting to get out of school or off work for the weekend? In those moments, the hands on the clock seem to move slower and slower and then stand still (or move backwards). But when we take our eyes off the clock for a while as we get occupied with the task at hand, time speeds up again and the moment we were waiting for arrives. When Shulamite was watching the clock she was overwhelmed by her feelings of separation from Solomon and her desire to be with him as his wife. But we must remember that God's restrictions are there for our benefit. We are assured by God that the blessing that awaits us in His timing is better than what we might abscond with today. The courtship period for Shulamite and Solomon, as well as for us, is intended to be its own special blessing and it is the blessing God has for us in that moment. Learning to live by faith requires us to accept that God's provision to us for the moment is sufficient—this is what it means to be content. To be discontented is to view God's provision to us for the moment as inadequate. Forfeiting future blessings for immediate flesh gratification is contrary to the Word and wisdom of God, and in fact, is how God defines a profane person. (Hebrews 12:16) Such a person misses out on God's best.

## Application Points

- **MAIN PRINCIPLE:** By God's design, the blessing of sexual pleasure is reserved for marriage and not to be absconded during courtship.

- During the courtship phase of a relationship, desiring to engage in lovemaking and feelings of separation resulting from boundaries in the relationship are normal feelings, but there is purpose for and satisfaction to be derived from the courtship without sex.

## Discussion Questions

1. Why does Shulamite dream that she is physically separated from Solomon?

2. Are there clues in the passage that the boundaries in place during the courtship phase are by mutual agreement of Solomon and Shulamite?

3. The passage pictures a changing of seasons from Fall to Spring, from courtship to marriage. What are the purposes of courtship and how might those purposes be better served without the couple engaging in premarital sex?

4. Why might Shulamite long to take Solomon to the very room where she was conceived? Is there a modern equivalent to Shulamite's emphasis on the location where they will engage in lovemaking?

5. Why does Shulamite call upon animals to witness her oath to the daughters of Jerusalem?

6. Why does the Song not offer advice to the sons of Jerusalem?

# Chapter 4

# Solomon Makes an Entrance

We have all heard someone say something like "so and so sure knows how to make an entrance." The word "entrance" is a theatrical term for making an appearance on stage, and when that is done in a way that commands the attention of the audience, the actor is said to have made an entrance. When I think of making an entrance I am always reminded of the Disney movie *Aladdin* in which the main character finds a genie and makes a wish to become a prince because he believes by doing so he can woo the affection of the princess. His wish is granted and the genie gives him an elephant to ride and an entourage of soldiers, musicians, dancers, and servants bearing gifts for the sultan. Aladdin made an entrance with his entourage and captivated the attention of the entire city and the sultan. In the Song of Solomon, while there is a reference to the "curtains of Solomon" in chapter 1, we are not formally introduced to Solomon by name until chapter 3. Given the Biblical account of

Solomon's wealth in 1 Kings 10—the Bible says he drank from vessels of gold and "none were of silver: it was nothing accounted of in the days of Solomon" and "Solomon exceeded all the kings of the earth for riches"—we should expect that when it was time to go receive his Shulamite and bring her to the wedding, he would make an entrance, and so he does. Solomon's entrance is not to win Shulamite but to declare her great value to him and celebrate their love as they travel to the wedding. This also provides the reader of the Song with the formal introduction of the groom, and symbolically, the blessing in store for those that follow God's wisdom for marriage.

## Scripture And Comments

The passage under study in this chapter (Song 3:6-4:7) brings us into the unit of the Song (3:6-5:1) addressing the consummation of the marriage. In addition, we are introduced to a new speaker in the Song that will be referred to herein as the narrator. The narrator's primary function in the Song, unlike the daughters who interact with Shulamite, is to formally introduce Solomon (3:6-3:11), then later Shulamite (6:10), and then the married couple (8:5). Although the narrator will call upon the daughters to watch Solomon's approaching caravan, the narrator also calls the audience's attention at critical times.

NARRATOR

Song 3:6 Who *is* this that cometh out of the wilderness

like pillars of smoke,

perfumed with myrrh and frankincense,

with all powders of the merchant?

<u>7</u> Behold his bed, which *is* Solomon's;

threescore valiant men *are* about it,

of the valiant of Israel.

<u>8</u> They all hold swords,

*being* expert in war:

every man *hath* his sword upon his thigh

because of fear in the night.

<u>9</u> King Solomon made himself a chariot

of the wood of Lebanon.

<u>10</u> He made the pillars thereof *of* silver,

the bottom thereof *of* gold,

the covering of it *of* purple,

the midst thereof being paved *with* love,

for the daughters of Jerusalem.

<u>11</u> Go forth, O ye daughters of Zion,

and behold king Solomon

with the crown wherewith his mother crowned him

in the day of his espousals,

and in the day of the gladness of his heart.

Shulamite's dream of separation from her lover, culminating with her charge to the daughters that sexual love is worth waiting for (3:1-5), is immediately followed by an end to the separation. The Song paints the picture of Solomon arriving in a wedding caravan to take Shulamite to the wedding feast. At the outset, it should be noted again that while it is possible that the Song records historical events, there is no reason to assume that to be the case. Some assume a historical record is intended because Solomon is mentioned by name and attested to be the author of the Song. But it could as easily be that Solomon, due to his fame and reputation, only functions as a character in the Song with whom the audience can readily identify. This device effectively conveys the great value of what Shulamite obtains by remaining sexually pure and waiting for the right person and the right time (i.e., within marriage) before engaging in sex. There is likewise no reason to assume Shulamite to be a real person as opposed to merely a character in the Song that young ladies can identify with and thus listen to her wisdom. In any event, history or not, the wisdom message remains the same.

In 3:6, the narrator is introduced, who asks the rhetorical question, **who is this that cometh out of the wilderness like pillars of smoke**. The question ostensibly calls for the attention of the **daughters of Jerusalem**, who are eager to get a glimpse of Solomon, but this is a device to call the audience's attention. The narrator compares the caravan to **pillars of smoke**. Just as **pillars of smoke** rise in the air, so also the caravan appears to rise as it ascends to where Shulamite is located (possibly Lebanon, see notes on 4:8). The caravan is **perfumed with myrrh and frankincense, with all powders of the merchant**. Recall that in 1:13, Shulamite referred to her lover as "a bundle of myrrh...[who will] lie all night betwixt my breasts." Her Solomon will later associate the fragrances of **myrrh** and **frankincense** with her breasts (4:6) and in general these fragrances are associated in the Song with lovemaking and sexuality (4:14, 5:1, 5:5, 5:13). The term **myrrh** refers to an aromatic gum (or resin) from the bark of a tree, which was expensive and imported into Israel. **Frankincense** refers to a fragrant resin. The visual image of **pillars** or billows **of smoke** is intensified when combined with the information about the aromatic fragrances. These fragrances are associated with sexuality and lovemaking, and the arriving caravan is seen as sending up such fragrant billows. Solomon arrives to get his bride and the time for consummation of the marriage is near.

Further focusing on the impending wedding consummation, the narrator draws **(behold)** the daughters' eyes (and ours) to **his bed, which is Solomon's.** The **bed** is not the sort of bed designed for a bedroom and sleep, but the royal traveling couch. Surrounding the portable **bed** or couch are **threescore** (sixty) **valiant** (mighty) **men...of the valiant of Israel.** These are Solomon's royal guards, and naturally, **they all hold swords, being expert in war; every man hath his sword upon his thigh because of fear in the night.** The apparent **fear in the night** would be bandits, and as Jewish wedding caravans typically arrived to pick up the bride in the evening, they would expect nighttime travel. That there is a concern about bandits implies that the caravan must travel a great distance to Shulamite, and this in turn further reinforces the imagery of distant separation prior to the marriage.

The narrator continues to provide fine details about the wedding coach. **King Solomon made himself a chariot of the wood of Lebanon.** The term **chariot** is the Hebrew *affiryon* and occurs only here in the entire Bible and does not mean a battle **chariot** but refers to the royal coach or palanquin, and possibly to a special coach made for the occasion. The Hebrew Mishnah uses this term to refer to a bridal litter. In any event, it is made of the **wood of**

**Lebanon,** most certainly the very best cedar wood available as Lebanon was famous for its cedars. Notably, Lebanon was the source for the cedars Solomon used to build the Temple. (1 Kings 5:6-9) It is further noteworthy that Solomon was known for his arboreal knowledge, and especially his knowledge of Lebanon's cedars. (1 Kings 4:33) As noted in the preface, this motif together with the Song's heavy focus on animals and flora with which Solomon was well studied support his authorship of the Song.

The narrator further explains that **the pillars** or posts were **made** (wood overlaid) in **silver**. The term **bottom** is the Hebrews *refidah* and occurs only here in the entire Bible and likely refers to either the support or back of the couch, and is wood **made of** (overlaid with) **gold**. The **seat** itself is upholstered (**the covering of it**) in **purple**, a color often associated with elegance and royalty. The interior of the coach is **paved** or inlaid **with love** (or lovingly) by (not **for**) **the daughters of Jerusalem**, apparently as a wedding gift to the couple.

The picture painted by the narrator is one of exquisite elegance. Solomon spared no expense and provided the very best for his beloved as a token of his love. But more than that, the caravan suggests the great value of their love. Shulamite's waiting is over and the arriving royal caravan confirms that what she will now enjoy was certainly worth waiting for, and in particular, her Solomon was worth waiting for. And the chorus is also witness to this. As the courtship formally ends and the wedding ritual begins, all of the feelings of separation and the seemingly endless waiting are justified, and the anticipation for this day will now be satiated. Had

Shulamite not waited for the right person and the right time, this valuable experience she now has would not have been the same.

The narrator instructs the **daughters of Zion** to **go forth** to meet the caravan as it arrives and to **behold** (gaze upon) **King Solomon with the crown wherewith his mother crowned him in the day of his espousals, and in the day of the gladness of his heart**. The chorus not only welcomes the caravan but their observation of Shulamite's blessing in her Solomon is instructive to them of the wisdom of waiting for the right person and right time. The **crown** is a special **crown** gifted to Solomon on his wedding day, which is not just any **day** but **the day of the gladness of his heart**, in other words, the best **day** ever because of the joy in **his heart**. This indicates that their marriage had the blessing of Solomon's **mother** Bathsheba, another validation of the core wisdom of the Song.

> SOLOMON
>
> Song 4:1 Behold, thou *art* fair, my love;
>
> behold, thou *art* fair;
>
> thou *hast* doves' eyes within thy locks:
>
> thy hair *is* as a flock of goats,
>
> that appear from mount Gilead.
>
> 2 Thy teeth *are* like a flock *of sheep that are even* shorn,
>
> which came up from the washing;
>
> whereof every one bear twins,
>
> and none *is* barren among them.
>
> 3 Thy lips *are* like a thread of scarlet,

and thy speech *is* comely:
thy temples *are* like a piece of a pomegranate
within thy locks.

4 Thy neck *is* like the tower of David
builded for an armoury, whereon there hang
a thousand bucklers,
all shields of mighty men.

5 Thy two breasts *are* like two young roes
that are twins, which feed among the lilies.

6 Until the day break,
and the shadows flee away,
I will get me to the mountain of myrrh,
and to the hill of frankincense.

7 Thou *art* all fair, my love;
*there is* no spot in thee.

The caravan arrived and now Solomon will describe the beauty of his Shulamite and his intense desire to make love to her. Note here that he only describes what he can see while she is clothed; later Solomon will describe Shulamite's beauty while she stands before him nude (7:1-9). She is **fair** or beautiful and she is **my love** and her **eyes** are **doves' eyes**, which is exactly what he said to her in 1:15. The precise meaning of her having **doves' eyes** is something we cannot be dogmatic about, but obviously Solomon complements the beauty of her eyes. What we can know is that these birds are white in coloration with striking **eyes** that typically have a bright orange pupil and black iris. Again, keep in mind that this is poetry and so he is not saying that his Shulamite has orange **eyes**. Instead, her **eyes** are a striking feature just as **doves' eyes**.

We do well to remember that Solomon was an accomplished ornithologist and so his repeated references to **doves' eyes** in the Song should not surprise us. (1 Kings 4:33)

Solomon then compares her **hair** to **a flock of goats, that appear from mount Gilead**, a mountain east of the Jordan River. Shulamite apparently has long, dark hair, and from a great distance, as a group of shaggy black goats descend the mountain, they provide an image of her hair. We see throughout the Song a high esteem for the beauty of nature and a prolific use of the natural elements (flowers, trees, and animals) to convey beauty as well as virility, and as already noted Solomon was a student of such things. (1 Kings 4:33) When the goats descend the mountain the shape formed by the herd changes, resembling her dark hair as she moves and as the wind blows. Further, Solomon commends Shulamite's teeth, and keeping in mind the lack of quality dental care in the ancient world, this would naturally be a stand out mark of beauty. Indeed, her **teeth are like a flock of sheep that are even shorn, which came up from the washing**; in other words, her teeth are white and even. Also, **every one** of her teeth **bear twins, and none is barren among them**, meaning she has no missing or broken teeth.

Solomon describes Shulamite's lips with a simile, **like a thread of scarlet**. He not only praises the beauty of her lips, but also the beauty of her voice as she speaks, for her **speech is comely**. Through or **within her locks** Solomon can see her **temples**, which are also praised with a simile, **like a piece** or slice **of a pomegranate**. The word **locks**, according to Strong's dictionary, could also be translated as "veil." Either way, the more difficult concept for us is likening her **temples** to a **pomegranate**, a complement he will repeat in 6:7. Most probably, he is not saying her **temples** physically resemble a **pomegranate**, but that even her temples are sexually alluring. The imagery of the **pomegranate** will be repeated in 4:13 ("thy plants are an orchard of pomegranates, with pleasant fruits"), 6:7 ("as a piece of a pomegranate are they temples"), 6:11 ("...to see whether the vine flourished and the pomegranates budded"), 7:12 ("let us see if the vine flourish...and the pomegranates bud forth: there will I give thee my loves"), and 8:2 ("I would cause thee to drink of spiced wine of the juice of my pomegranate"). The **pomegranate** was considered an aphrodisiac in the ancient world, and throughout the Song it is used to convey a readiness of the body for lovemaking. And so here as well, his Shulamite is so beautiful that even her **temples** are alluring.

Solomon next describes her **neck** as being **like the tower of David builded for an armoury, whereon there hang a thousand bucklers, all shields of mighty men**. The imagery of a **tower** pictures both strength as well as beauty and suggests her neck is long and slender. We find a similar description in 7:4 of strength and beauty ("thy neck is as a tower of ivory"). Probably the phrase **builded for an armoury** pictures a stone or brick reinforcement, which likely refers to jewels Shulamite wears for her wedding, for instance, a necklace of stones. Solomon describes her neck with reference to a defensive **tower** covered with the soldiers' **shields** with their different colors and designs blending together like jewelry.

Shulamite's **breasts are like two young roes** or gazelles **that are twins** and **feed among the lilies**. Again, Solomon describes her clothed, although he will repeat the complement again in 7:3 where the context plainly shows he is describing her unclothed. Like prior descriptions he makes a visual comparison (e.g., flock of goats to her hair). The comparison here is two **young** gazelles identical in appearance standing near one another feeding and well-nourished on the **lilies**. These are not only beautiful and graceful animals, but they are **young** and full of life. By comparison, her **breasts** reflect the same youthful beauty. Because he compares her **breasts** to gazelles feeding (nourished) he may be commending their size as well.

In view of all that he sees, Solomon anticipates their sexual union as the marriage is consummated and expresses that he will make love to her **until the day break, and the shadows flee away**, that is, until morning. Recall that in 2:17, Shulamite invited Solomon to make love to her: "Until the day break, and the shadows flee away, turn, my beloved, and be thou like a roe or a young hart upon the mountains of Bether." As pointed out in the notes to 2:17, the "mountains of Bether" referred to Shulamite's breasts. Thus in 4:6, Solomon accepts the invitation of 2:17. Connection points like 2:17 and 4:6 demonstrate the unity of the Song.

Having just complemented the beauty of her **breasts**, he states his intent to make love to her by reference to touching her **breasts** just as he was earlier invited to do, which he describes metaphorically as **the mountain of myrrh, and...the hill of frankincense**. As noted previously, the term **myrrh** refers to an aromatic gum (or resin) from the bark of a tree, which was expensive and imported into Israel. **Frankincense** refers to a fragrant resin that Shulamite would likely apply (or wear in a pouch, see notes on 1:13) near her breasts, and her scent attracts him. There is a figure of speech here (metonymy) in that a phrase is representative of another word or phrase with which it is associated. Solomon's reference to touching her breasts is metonymy for the entire act of lovemaking that they will engage in that very night. Solomon's summary assessment of his bride, forming an *inclusio* with his opening words in 4:1, is that she is **all fair**, in other words, beautiful in every detail. He affectionately calls her **my love** as he does repeatedly in the Song (e.g., 1:15, 2:2, 2:10, 2:13, 4:1). She is without any blemish at all (**no spot in thee**) in Solomon's eyes.

Putting all the pieces together, then, Solomon with the royal caravan in all its elegance arrived to pick up Shulamite. The caravan portends the beauty and value of their love that is theirs to enjoy because Shulamite guarded her sexual purity, but also, the great effort Solomon made to create the coach shows what a fine and affectionate husband Shulamite found (recall from the introduction, "the upright love thee"). Solomon is wholly pleased in his bride, viewing and verbalizing her clothed beauty as she is arrayed for the wedding, and accepts her earlier invitation to make love, which will occur after the ceremony.

## Closing

Solomon is not the only one in the passage to have made an entrance. One thing preachers who routinely do weddings will often say about them is that the bride is always radiant. This is her special day and an enormous effort goes into every detail from the shoes to the dress, the jewelry to the veil, the hair and nails, etc. And

Shulamite was no exception. As elegant as Solomon's palanquin was, and as attention getting as his caravan, surely those things were no match for his Shulamite on this special day. Her beauty is everything he expected and more. Shulamite made an entrance and commanded Solomon's full attention as she dazzled and delighted him. While the Song seems to generally express itself from the perspective of Shulamite and the value to Shulamite of a proper courtship and waiting to engage in a sexual relationship until marriage, we see plainly that Solomon also recognizes the great value he receives in his Shulamite. She has made an entrance in his life as the spotless one and he adores and treasures her.

## Application Points

- **MAIN PRINCIPLE:** When through a courtship with proper sexual boundaries the right person to marry is found, the wait for the marriage will be more than justified and the anticipation more than satisfied when the marriage day finally arrives.

- The proper courtship resulted in Shulamite finding a husband of exceptional quality.

- We should verbalize the qualities of our spouse, which means we must take notice of those qualities and not take them for granted.

## Discussion Questions

1. What is the role of the narrator in the passage?

2. Why is so much time devoted to the description of Solomon's caravan?

3. Why does the narrator call upon the daughters to watch and greet the caravan?

4. Why do you think the narrator mentions Solomon's mother?

5. Solomon describes his Shulamite's beauty in detail. What about the circumstances makes his description especially important?

6. What do you think Solomon means when he says "there is no spot in thee"?

# Chapter 5

# The Lovers United

One of the doctrines the Bible teaches that is often overlooked is what we might call a "theology of waiting." The fact is that we despise waiting. If we have to wait, then something is wrong or unfair. It rarely occurs to us that God has His reasons and waiting might yield a better result than immediate gratification. One of the best "waiting" examples is in John 11. When Jesus "heard therefore that [Lazarus] was sick, he abode two days still in the same place where he was." (John 11:6) Only after Lazarus succumbed to his illness and died did Jesus leave to Bethany. When he arrived, he was met by Lazarus' sister Martha who remarked, "if thou hadst been here, my brother had not died." (John 11:21) When Jesus subsequently met Mary at the gravesite, she said, "if thou hadst been here, my brother had not died." (John 11:32) Mary, Martha, and the other mourners believed Jesus was four days late and therefore could not bring healing to Lazarus, but of course God is never late. Jesus delayed his arrival for his divine purposes, and we have to come to understand that there are a number of things in life where God does not say yes or no, but wait, and often we cannot comprehend why.

I am convinced that many times when God tells us to wait, it is to show us that what we think we need most, we really do not need. And the waiting allows for God to show us His hand of blessing beyond what we imagined. In the area of marriage and sex, God says, "trust me and wait." What the Song assures us now, as the marriage is finally consummated, is that in this area of life, God has honored the waiting by providing an enduring abundance. The time of waiting (the courtship) had a purpose as it allowed the non-physical elements of the relationship to form and strengthen on grounds other than the physical, and this in turn makes what remains to be shared in the marriage better.

## Scripture And Comments

We saw in 4:1-7 that Solomon praised Shulamite's beauty and expressed his desire to make love to her. The courtship has come to an end and so now Solomon can invite Shulamite to join him. Early portions of the Song focused on Shulamite's feelings of separation during the courtship, which were visualized through imagery of physical separation and even of Shulamite searching for Solomon. It is fitting now at the transition point between the courtship and the marriage that Solomon would acknowledge their prior separation, again using the imagery of physical distance, as he beckons Shulamite to himself.

SOLOMON

<u>Song 4:8</u> Come with me from Lebanon, *my* spouse,

with me from Lebanon:

look from the top of Amana,

from the top of Shenir and Hermon,

from the lions' dens,

from the mountains of the leopards.

<u>9</u> Thou hast ravished my heart, my sister, *my* spouse;

thou hast ravished my heart with one of thine eyes,

with one chain of thy neck.

<u>10</u> How fair is thy love, my sister, *my* spouse!

how much better is thy love than wine!

and the smell of thine ointments than all spices!

<u>11</u> Thy lips, O *my* spouse, drop *as* the honeycomb:

honey and milk *are* under thy tongue;

and the smell of thy garments *is* like the smell of Lebanon.

<u>12</u> A garden inclosed *is* my sister, *my* spouse;

a spring shut up, a fountain sealed.

<u>13</u> Thy plants *are* an orchard of pomegranates,

with pleasant fruits;

camphire, with spikenard,

<u>14</u> Spikenard and saffron; calamus and cinnamon,

with all trees of frankincense;

myrrh and aloes,

with all the chief spices:

<u>15</u> A fountain of gardens,

a well of living waters,

and streams from Lebanon.

Solomon invites his Shulamite to himself (to join him in lovemaking) in a way that acknowledges the prior boundaries of their courtship with words connoting physical distance and separation: **Come with me from Lebanon, my spouse, with me from Lebanon.** Many expositors understand Shulamite to be **from Lebanon**, and that interpretation is plausible. The difficulty is that much of the Song is figurative, and if we take this line literally, then should not we also take the rest of the verse literally? Solomon calls upon Shulamite to **look** or descend **from the top of** Mount **Amana, from the top of** Mount **Shenir and** Mount **Hermon, from the lions' dens, from the mountains of the leopards.** On a map and through the lens of modern transportation, **Lebanon** is only a short distance from Israel (or Jerusalem), but not so when traveling by foot or carriage. Obviously, Shulamite did not live on all these mountaintops (all located in **Lebanon**) nor in **lions' dens** (i.e., mountain caves) or among **leopards.** The better view is that the purpose of this language, including the reference to **Lebanon**, is to convey through poetic terms Shulamite's complete inaccessibility to Solomon as a lover during the courtship.

Solomon continues his plea for Shulamite to join him by explaining that she **hast ravished** or stolen his **heart.** Shulamite has his complete affection so that he refers to her not only as **my spouse** but also by the term of endearment common in ancient Egyptian love poetry, **my sister.** He goes further and explains that Shulamite **hast ravished** or stolen his **heart with one** glance **of** her **eyes, even with one chain of** her **neck.** She had his heart at the moment he glimpsed her **eyes** and at the moment he saw just a jewel on a necklace around her **neck.** Solomon remarks **how fair** or delightful **is** her **love** for him. Again he refers to her as **my sister** and **my spouse**. These are not sexually charged terms (the **love** is not the Hebrew *dod* that usually denotes sexual love in the Song), but terms of affection, and it is critical that we understand as we read Solomon's praises throughout the Song that his words are sourced in his affection for her. In the next line, Solomon again uses the Hebrew *dod* when he says, **how much better is** Shulamit's **love than wine**. Recall that Shulamite said in 1:2 of Solomon that his "love is better than wine." They each recognize the figuratively intoxicating effects of their physical pleasures, meaning that just as wine affects the entire body, the pleasure they may enjoy is complete. Just as Shulamite's lovemaking is superior to wine, so also **the smell of** her **ointments** is better **than all spices**. Her fragrant **ointments** arouse Solomon's sense of smell more than any other fragrance, and those **ointments** serve as an extension of her physical beauty and pleasures.

Solomon next describes the pleasure of kissing his **spouse** or bride Shulamite, for her **lips... drop sweetness like the honeycomb** and **honey and milk are under** her **tongue**. To use a modern term, this is foreplay as Solomon will proceed to make love to Shulamite. As he kisses her and begins removing her clothes he remarks that even **the smell of** her **garments** (her clothes) is superior, **like the smell of Lebanon**, meaning a **smell** that is exotic and uncommon. Then, critical to the overall wisdom teaching of the Song, Solomon says, **a garden inclosed is my sister my spouse**. To make love to Shulamite is to enter her **garden**. She is a virgin and so she is described as a **garden inclosed**. The imagery is that there is a fence or wall about her **garden** with a locked gate, to which

Solomon will be the first and the only to enter. Similarly, she is **a spring shut up** and **a fountain sealed**. Recall that in Proverbs 5:15-18, Solomon used the imagery of a "cistern," "fountains," "rivers" and "running waters" as metaphors for sexual pleasures within marriage. As a virgin, Shulamite's sexual pleasures (**fountain**) have not been experienced by anyone.

As Solomon figuratively begins to enter Shulamite's **garden** for the first time, he uses imagery we would expect of a garden. Her **plants are an orchard of pomegranates, with pleasant fruits**. Keeping in mind that **pomegranates** were associated with sexual pleasures in the ancient world, Solomon's point as he beholds and caresses Shulamite's **garden** (i.e., her nude body) that is filled with an entire **orchard** full of **pomegranates** is that the sexual experience with her will be totally satisfying because of the abundance. Her **garden** has **pleasant** fruits. In a real **garden**, an abundance of fruits to eat is the hallmark of a **garden** that completely serves its purpose of providing sustenance. Here, Shulamite's sexual **garden** (her body from the perspective of sexual pleasure) provides those sexual pleasures in abundance. Having appealed to the senses of sight and taste, Solomon next describes the experience by appealing to the sense of smell; he finds pleasant fragrances there of **camphire** or henna blossoms, **spikenard** (a fragrant ointment) **and saffron** (a spice from a fragrant flower), **calamus** (a fragrant plant) **and cinnamon** and **all trees of frankincense** (a fragrant gum resin derived from a tree); **myrrh** (a sweet smelling substance from trees) **and aloes, with all the chief spices**. These fragrances are an extension of her sexuality, reaching to his senses, arousing and beckoning him. Again the focus is on abundance so that he will be wholly satisfied in his lovemaking with Shulamite.

Following that same theme, but returning to the "fountain" imagery of 4:12, Solomon says in 4:15 that Shulamite is **a fountain of gardens, a well of living waters, and streams from** the mountains **Lebanon**. Abundant waters would make the garden lush and sustaining. There is an abounding and sustaining supply of sexual pleasures to be enjoyed with Shulamite, not only on their wedding night, but throughout their marriage as he will return again and again to the inexhaustible pleasures of her **garden**.

> SHULAMITE
>
> <u>16</u> Awake, O north wind;
>
> and come, thou south;
>
> blow upon my garden,
>
> *that* the spices thereof may flow out.
>
> Let my beloved come into his garden,
>
> and eat his pleasant fruits.

Responding to Solomon's initiation of lovemaking, and especially his figurative entrance into her **garden**, Shulamite is now completely available to him. Whereas she has to this point been "a garden inclosed" (a virgin), the **garden** is now available. She calls upon the **north wind** to **awake** and the **south** wind as well, to **blow upon** her **garden that the spices thereof may flow out**. The aromatic fragrances of her **garden** irresistibly pull Solomon in as it is now the appropriate time for lovemaking. Solomon described what he saw and what he could smell in the garden, and now Shulamite invites him to enjoy those pleasures when she says, **let my**

**beloved come into his garden.** Her body (**garden**) is no longer only her (**my**) **garden**, but now **his garden** as well. Within marriage, as Paul confirms in the New Testament, each one's body is not their own, but belongs to their spouse: "The wife hath not power of her own body, but the husband: and likewise also the husband hath not power of his own body, but the wife." (I Corinthians 7:4) Before he could only see the **garden** (e.g., 4:13) but now he can freely partake of it as his, and thus we read the invitation to **eat his pleasant fruits**.

SOLOMON

<u>Song 5:1</u> I am come into my garden, my sister, *my* spouse:

I have gathered my myrrh with my spice;

I have eaten my honeycomb with my honey;

I have drunk my wine with my milk:

Solomon confirms that he has **come into my garden**, calling upon Shulamite as **my sister, my spouse**. Again, the use of **sister** is a term of affection and endearment in the Song. (Song 4:9-10, 12; 5:2) Solomon confirms his entire satisfaction in making love with Shulamite and consummating their marriage. He states that he has **gathered** his **myrrh with** his **spice, eaten my honeycomb with my honey**, and **drunk** his **wine with** his **milk**. Notice that the fruits and fragrances of her **garden** that were previously hers are now his. What he found in her is all that he anticipated, recalling the earlier imagery: honeycomb and honey (4:11), myrrh (4:6, 14), wine (4:10) and milk (4:11). As before, we should not attempt to construe from language like **eaten my honeycomb** precisely what the lovers have done. That is not at all the point of this language. They made love and Solomon was fully satisfied.

> NARRATOR
>
> eat, O friends;
>
> drink, yea, drink abundantly, O beloved.

The narrator calls upon the couple's **friends** at the wedding feast to celebrate their love, to **eat** and **drink**. The narrator then calls upon the newly married couple (the **beloved**) to **drink abundantly**, meaning to physically enjoy one another to the fullest.


## Closing

Back when movies were in black and white, the stories often presented love, romance and marriage. However, the way Hollywood of yesteryear presented these themes was a far cry from the gratuitous skin of today's films. Those old films would present a couple embracing, and then one of the lovers would reach out and close the bedroom door, implying what they would do but not inviting us into their bedroom to watch them. Or we would see a silhouette through the window and blinds, and after the couple embraced, the lights would be turned off. We knew what was going to happen but telling the story did not require that we witness their lovemaking. The Song likewise leads up to the lovemaking and tells us it happens, but does not delve into gratuitous or crass details. The Song is erotic, but conveys these elements poetically. The Song does not purport to be a "how to" manual nor are such specific details important. The Song is much more concerned about conveying their mutual passion, the qualitative sense of the experience, and the wisdom of reserving sexual experience for the right person within marriage. This brings us into the Song so that we can rejoice in what Shulamite and Solomon have.

## Application Points

- **MAIN PRINCIPLE:** Remaining sexually pure for marriage will provide an abundance of sexual pleasures to be enjoyed throughout the marriage.

- Sexual pleasure within marriage is intended to be mutual pleasing and mutually consented, but otherwise the Song does not express restrictions for lovemaking.

## Discussion Questions

1. Is 4:8 to be construed literally or poetically?

2. Does Shulamite's purity matter to Solomon? Why?

3. What is suggested by the abundance and variety of flora and fragrances in Shulamite's garden?

4. What is suggested by there being a fountain in the garden?

5. In 4:16, Shulamite appears to not only be willing, but inviting and responsive to Solomon. If a wife is willing but uninviting and unresponsive, what message does that send to her husband?

6. If a wife is inviting and responsive, what message does that send to her husband?

7. If a husband is uninviting and unresponsive, what message does that send to his wife?

# Chapter 6

# A Time to Marry

When people are young, they cannot grow up quick enough. And then when they are older they usually reminisce fondly of their childhood. Some people even wish they could get a "do over" of their childhood knowing the wisdom they obtained as adults. Solomon wisely wrote that "[t]o every thing there is a season, and a time for every purpose under the heaven: A time to be born, and a time to die...A time to get, and a time to lose; a time to keep, and a time to cast away...A time to love, and a time to hate." (Ecclesiastes 3:1-8) His point was that life has an order to it that is for the most part out of our control and we must learn to enjoy the blessings of God in the moment and not get caught up on what we cannot change. Yet, as the transitions in life come, there are uncertainties about the future that can bring anxiety, and at the same time we may experience the loss of that which we must leave behind.

For Shulamite, who for some years was a young lady among the daughters of Jerusalem, eager to grow up and marry and (most probably) raise a family, that "daughters of Jerusalem" period of her life will imminently come to an end. The unique experiences and pleasures of being a young single lady (likely in her teen years) will shortly trail away into the past forever, and her life will dramatically change as she becomes the wife of Solomon. The consummation of the marriage that Shulamite longs for is also the pivot point of this portion of her life as she leaves the daughters behind and moves forward as wife to Solomon. As she takes on what is in some sense a new identity, new adventures and blessings await, but she must leave some things behind. Thus, we find Shulamite reminiscing about her life before marriage and the inner turmoil she experienced as the wedding day approached.

## Scripture And Comments

We previously saw one and possibly two dream sequences in the Song. (Song 2:9-14; 3:1-4) Both sequences related to Shulamite's feelings of separation during the courtship and her longing to be united in marriage to Solomon. The dream sequence in Song 5:2-8 has similarities to the dream in 3:1-4 (e.g., searching for Solomon in the city, meeting the guards), but unlike earlier where she is separated from Solomon, here Solomon comes to her (as he did in 2:9-14) and she initially rejects his overtures. As we consider the meaning of these verses, it is important to note not only the similarities but the differences from the earlier sequences. Further, we must keep in mind that the Song presents a series of reminiscences and is not rigidly chronological. We should not assume that 5:2 temporally follows 5:1, but instead must drill down on the context and language to understand where 5:2-8 fits chronologically in the events relayed to us in the Song.

### SHULAMITE

Song 5:2 I sleep, but my heart waketh:

*it is* the voice of my beloved that knocketh, *saying,*

In Song 5:2-8, we again find Shulamite searching for her Solomon, as we did in 1:7-8 and 3:1-4. As already noted, the difference here is that she drives him away before going to search for him. Many expositors take this dream sequence to reflect a subsequent marriage problem where Shulamite takes Solomon for granted and turns a cold shoulder toward his sexual advances, but after spurning him, she quickly regrets her conduct and searches for him. This view stems from assuming the Song presents a chronological sequence of events (i.e., that this passage must relate a post-wedding event) and a hermeneutic that takes the text in an overly literal fashion at the expense of not taking into proper account the poetic elements of the Song. It seems apparent that if they were married and she resisted his advances so that he was locked out of their bedroom, he would simply go to another room to sleep. Solomon would not need to go hide in the city or flee the city, nor would the guards dare assault Solomon's wife. We must remember that this is a dream sequence where what unfolds is neither literal (it does not reflect an actual historic event but a dream) nor entirely rational, and indeed if the Song intended it to be literal there is no purpose served by wrapping the events in a dream sequence. Rather, the dream through its poetic elements reveals Shulamite's subconscious turmoil. Like the earlier sequences where she searched for

Solomon, she is burdened by the boundaries in place as she anticipates their wedding and the physical consummation of their love. But here, the dream also reflects Shulamite's apprehension about the coming wedding, which for her will be in some ways a rite of passage, a transition from being among the daughters of Jerusalem to belonging wholly to her husband and leaving behind forever that season of her life when she was among the daughters.

Shulamite says, **I sleep, but my heart** (my mind) **waketh**, meaning that although asleep her mind is active, i.e., in a dream. She hears **the voice of** her **beloved that knocketh** on the door to her room, and then he speaks to her. In other words, she dreams of being awakened from slumber by Solomon, which possibly parallels 2:10.

SOLOMON

Open to me, my sister, my love,

my dove, my undefiled:

for my head is filled with dew,

*and* my locks with the drops of the night.

After knocking on Shulamite's door, Solomon implicitly expresses his desire for sex. If this were their marriage bedroom, we would not expect him to be locked out regardless of whether Shulamite wanted to have sex. But again, this is a dream. He says to her, **open to me, my sister, my love, my dove, my undefiled**. The term **undefiled** speaks of perfect moral piety, and is used of Job, whom God described as "a perfect and an upright man." (Job 1:8, 2:3) He tells her that his **head is filled with dew** and his **locks with the drops of the night**. The point is that he traveled some distance at night, likely into the early morning, in the wet outside air, to be with her. This imagery again suggests their separation as before (e.g., 1:7-8), and thus points to a time prior to the wedding during their courtship. Up until now, Shulamite longed for nothing but to be with her lover, but as the next verse will show, she resists him. It is at this point that many expositors give too little attention to the fact that all this happens in a dream and that it parallels the earlier searches for Solomon. Taking it as a literal historical event that happened, some infer that Solomon essentially returned late from the office hoping to find a warm bed, but finds the "honeymoon is over" and not only is he going to bed unhappy, he does not even get to sleep in his own bed. But this creates problems like explaining why he had to travel through the night hours to get to her, why their shared bedroom would be locked to him, presumably in his own castle, and why he flees the castle and perhaps the city after being rejected rather than "sleeping on the couch."

A key word here is **undefiled**. Shulamite has "no spot" (4:7), is "a garden inclosed," "spring shut up," "fountain sealed" (4:12) and "a wall" (8:10). It is also helpful to be cognizant of the earlier emphasis on their separation, which was indicative not so much of being physically removed from one another but of the sexual boundaries between them until their wedding. We also saw that Shulamite anticipated with joy the day when Solomon would show up with the wedding caravan and escort her to the wedding, which would culminate in their consummation of their marriage. In this scene, Solomon bridged the distance between them through long travel, perhaps day and night, so that he can make love to her where she is rather than with a caravan to escort her to the wedding ceremony. The door to her bedchamber is locked, indicative of her sexual purity. But Solomon is ready to open the door and this causes anxiety for Shulamite and she makes excuses for not opening the door.

SHULAMITE

3 I have put off my coat;

how shall I put it on?

I have washed my feet;

how shall I defile them?

4 My beloved put in his hand by the hole *of the door,*

and my bowels were moved for him.

5 I rose up to open to my beloved;

and my hands dropped *with* myrrh,

and my fingers *with* sweet smelling myrrh,

upon the handles of the lock.

6 I opened to my beloved;

but my beloved had withdrawn himself, *and* was gone:

my soul failed when he spake:

I sought him, but I could not find him;

I called him, but he gave me no answer.

7 The watchmen that went about the city found me,

they smote me, they wounded me;

the keepers of the walls

took away my veil from me.

8 I charge you, O daughters of Jerusalem,

if ye find my beloved,

that ye tell him, that I *am* sick of love.

In response to Solomon's advances, Shulamite offers petty, irrational excuses such as **I have put off my coat; how shall I put it on?** In other words, her response to his plea for sex is that she is scantily clad and does not want to have to put her robe back on. Surely her lack of clothes is not an obstacle to his plans. She also says, **I have washed my feet; how shall I defile them?** In other words, she does not want to get dust on her feet on the way to the door. Again, it is unlikely that Solomon would be discouraged by her dusty feet. These irrational excuses for not opening her door reflect Shulamite's inner turmoil about the consummation of the marriage and the dramatic life changes for her on the other side of the wedding. On the one hand, she looks forward to it with great anticipation, but on the other, she has certain fears and apprehension as she will be leaving behind a season of life and entering into a new season of life, to which will be no turning back. What unfolds is that her anticipation wins over the fears and her determination to be with Solomon only strengthens.

As the scene progresses, her **beloved put in his hand by the hole of the door.** The **hole** is probably a latch hole or key hole where one might try to slide a hand through to move the lock. As noted in the translation notes of the NET Bible, the term **hand** (Hebrew *yad*) can be used euphemistically for the male sex organ, as reflected in some translations of Isaiah 57:8, 10 and in the Ugaritic and Qumran literature. This scene is quite possibly (and I think probably) a setting in which a double entendre is intended by these words. Solomon's attempt to open the door is symbolic of his attempt to make love with Shulamite. No ill intent should be ascribed to Solomon, for he cannot help what Shulamite dreams about. Rather, it is her feelings that we must grapple with. In response to his overture, her **bowels** or feelings (or emotions) **were moved for him**. As her feelings changed, she **rose up** from her bed **to open** her door for her **beloved**, her **hands dropped with myrrh**, and her **fingers** also dripped **with sweet smelling myrrh, upon the handles of the lock**. The poetic reference to aromatic myrrh was previously made in 1:13, 4:6, 4:14, and 5:1 with a sexual connotation; Shulamite's breast was the "mountain of myrrh" (Song 4:6) and Solomon referred to making love to Shulamite as having gathered "my myrrh with my spice." Obviously, there is no reason for Shulamite who has turned in for the evening to have her hand covered with myrrh, but in this dream sequence where emotions are intended and things needs not be literally understood, the **door**, his **hand**, and the **myrrh** all convey the suggestion of a sexual union that is first rebuffed but then accepted after her **bowels were moved**, albeit too late.

Shulamite once again finds herself searching for Solomon. She **opened** the door to her **beloved but** her **beloved had withdrawn himself and was gone**. Having failed to get to the door in time, her **soul failed** and when she **sought him** and **could not find him**, she **called him, but he gave no answer**. Solomon's hastened disappearance further indicates the surreal dream nature of this passage. As she did in the prior dream sequence (3:1-4), she goes about the city to find Solomon and runs into the night **watchmen that go about the city**. Indeed, the language of 5:7 (**the watchmen that went about the city found me**) exactly matches the first line of 3:3, providing yet another "connection point" demonstrating the robust unity of the Song. But this time, the guards **smote** her and **wounded** her. She calls them **the keepers of the walls** and explains that they **took away my veil** or cloak **from me**. Obviously, if she were married to Solomon or even to be wed to him, the guards would never beat her. But again, this is a dream sequence where the events are symbolic rather than literal. The term **walls** is used again in 8:9-10 as a symbol of Shulamite's sexual purity. The **watchmen** represent authority and they guard the wall, i.e., her purity, as did her brothers (8:8-9). The removal of her cloak and the beating are a harsh reminder of the boundaries in place until her and Solomon are married.

Shulamite now appeals to the **daughters of Jerusalem** that if they **find** her **beloved** that they tell **him that** she is **sick of love**, an expression she stated in 2:5 to describe her overwhelming anticipation of making love to Solomon for the first time. Recall that in 1:7 she appealed to the **daughters** to help her find Solomon. Here, she does not ask where he is, but only that they communicate a message on her behalf, that she is **sick of love** or "lovesick." She is faint with her anticipation and longing to be united with her Solomon as husband and wife, which indicates that she has mentally put behind her whatever fears or apprehension she had about the transition to married life that were poetically described within the dream sequence by her initially rejecting Solomon's advances.

DAUGHTERS

9 What *is* thy beloved more than *another* beloved, O thou fairest among women?

what *is* thy beloved more than *another* beloved,
that thou dost so charge us?

In response to Shulamite's search for Solomon and her charge to the daughters to relay a message to him that she is **sick of** or faint with **love**, the daughters ask her, **what is thy beloved more than another beloved, O thou fairest among women?** And in like vain, **what is thy beloved more than another beloved, that thou dost so charge us?** In the vernacular, what is so special about this man that you have troubled us to relay a message to him? Shulamite will answer their question, and after doing so, the daughters will volunteer to assist in the search.

SHULAMITE

10 My beloved *is* white and ruddy,
the chiefest among ten thousand.

11 His head *is as* the most fine gold,
his locks *are* bushy, *and* black as a raven.

12 His eyes *are* as *the eyes* of doves
by the rivers of waters,
washed with milk,
*and* fitly set.

13 His cheeks *are* as a bed of spices,
*as* sweet flowers:
his lips *like* lilies,
dropping sweet smelling myrrh.

14 His hands *are as* gold rings
set with the beryl:
his belly *is as* bright ivory
overlaid *with* sapphires.

<u>15</u> His legs *are as* pillars of marble,
set upon sockets of fine gold:
his countenance *is* as Lebanon,
excellent as the cedars.
<u>16</u> His mouth *is* most sweet:
yea, he *is* altogether lovely.
This *is* my beloved, and this *is* my friend,
O daughters of Jerusalem.

With great affection in her words, Shulamite responds to the daughters defending the uniqueness and fine features of Solomon. She begins with a summary statement and then describes his features from head to foot. She refers to her Solomon as her **beloved**, who is **white and ruddy**. The term **white** is the Hebrew *tsakh*, which Strong's defines as "dazzling, i.e., sunny, bright, (figuratively) evidence:--clear, dry, plainly, white." Given that this statement is a summary of the description that follows, which paints a portrait of Solomon using allusions to gold and gems, the idea of "dazzling" is likely intended. Her Solomon is **the chiefest** or finest **among ten thousand** men. Indeed, **his head is as the most fine gold** and **his locks** (hair) **are busty** or curly **and black as a raven.** As we have emphasized throughout, the Song is poetry, and this is extraordinarily clear in these words. To try to take the text in too wooden a sense rather than recognizing the poetic use of a simile (**as the most fine gold**) would make no sense at all. In her view, he is the very finest specimen of a man from head to toe so that she can describe him in terms of valuable elements and materials that the greatest artisans would use in their finest craftsmanship. She will also describe the finer features of his exquisite **head**, but she starts with the overall picture, a **head** like **gold** with curly **black** hair.

Solomon's **eyes are as the eyes of doves by the rivers of waters, washed with milk, and fitly set.** Expositors struggle with this imagery and the suggestions are without number, but perhaps the verse suffers from being overanalyzed. These birds are white in coloration with striking **eyes** that typically have a bright orange pupil and black iris. Again, keep in mind that this is a simile (note the use of **as**) and Shulamite is not saying her lover has orange **eyes**. The bright coloration of the doves' pupils is consistent with her summary description that Solomon is **white** (dazzling, a Hebrew term often used to describe shiny jewels or rocks) and her further use of gold, gems and jewels to describe him, and the bright orange of **the eyes of doves** are not unlike a bright gem. His **eyes** are a striking feature just **as the eyes of doves.** In particular, she speaks of **doves by the rivers of waters, washed with milk.** The **doves** appear **washed with milk** when they bathe because of their bright white coloration, which fits as a description of the sclera (white part) of Solomon's eyes. Also, his eyes are **fitly set** or mounted on his face, like jewels.

Again with a simile, Shulamite describes Solomon's **cheeks...as a bed of spices, as sweet flowers.** The language translated **bed of spices** refers to a garden terrace or landscaped garden bed, a luxury item in the ancient world. The **spices** yield a **sweet** aroma like **flowers.** The Song over and again uses garden imagery to describe some or all of the lovers' physical bodies to convey beauty through the lens of God's living handiwork (recall Matthew 6:28-29: "Consider the lilies of the field, how they grow; they toil not, neither do they spin: And yet I say unto you, That even Solomon in all his glory was not arrayed like one of these."). These similes do not allow us to quantitatively assess Solomon's features, nor to paint his portrait. Rather, Shulamite's poetic description is qualitative, describing his jeweled beauty through her eyes. Not only are his **eyes** striking but his **lips** are to be compared to **lilies, dropping sweet smelling myrrh**. Of course, the animals alluded to in the Song feed on the lilies (4:5) as does Solomon (6:3). Insofar as **myrrh** has continually been referred to conveying sexuality (myrrh being an ancient world aphrodisiac), his **lips** are inviting to be kissed and enjoyed.

Working her way down from his facial features, her Solomon has **hands** like **gold rings set with the beryl**. The point, of course, is not that his **hands** reflect these colors, any more than his head is actually "gold" in color. Rather, his hands are the finest work of the master artisan (ultimately, of course, that artisan is God himself). Similarly, **his belly is as bright ivory overlaid with sapphires**. Just as we should not take the description of his **hands** or head to literally describe their color as **gold**, we need not take **his belly** to be **ivory** white. Rather, the muscular features of his belly are likened to the fine craftsmanship of a master jeweler. Possibly the **bright ivory** reflects smoothness and the well-developed abdominal muscles are like the **sapphires**, but again, we must tread with caution in trying to turn the poetic description into a photograph.

Solomon's **legs are as pillars of marble**, a picture of beauty and strength, **set upon sockets of fine gold**. Marble columns or **pillars** always have a base (like a round column affixed atop a square or rectangular base), and here that quality base is overlaid **of fine gold,** a reference to his finely crafted feet. Every feature of Solomon, head to foot, is to be likened to the finest craftsmanship in jewels and architecture. Indeed, **his countenance** or facial appearance **is as Lebanon, excellent as the cedars. Lebanon** was known for its beauty and especially for its mighty **cedars.** These trees reflect the natural beauty and handiwork of God, strength, stability and height, all features of Solomon's overall presence. Keep in mind, as noted earlier, Solomon's special wisdom and knowledge concerning the cedars of Lebanon; that he would rely on this imagery is unsurprising. Shulamite adds that **his mouth is most sweet** and **he is altogether lovely** (delightful, an object of desire). He is desirable to kiss and to gaze upon.

Shulamite's description of her Solomon was in response to the daughters' question about what was so special about him that they should relay a message to him on her behalf. Her description fits the bill for what they asked, and when she finishes, Shulamite says to the daughters, **this is my beloved, and this is my friend** or companion, **O daughters of Jerusalem.** He is both the object of her love and her best **friend.** Solomon spoke at length in the Proverbs on the topic of friends (sometimes translated neighbors), and in particular, the value of a true friend, a relationship that entails a level of trust. (e.g., Proverbs 17:17: "A friend loveth at all times...."). The Song presents a couple who are best friends before they are lovers, as it should be, for it is only in such a relationship that non-sexual intimacy may flourish. As her friend, she wholly trusts him as she commits her life to him in marriage.

## Closing

We all know about "water cooler" talk. This is where the gossip train drives through the station and sometimes where the dirty laundry is hung to dry and frustrations are vented. It may be about another co-worker or a boss or a spouse. I have several times experienced being privy (by overhearing) water cooler talk that devolves into several women talking about the bad qualities of their significant other (usually husband) as they compete for who can describe the worst husband. Of course, in almost every instance, their husband is exactly today who they married years ago. What I have more often seen women do behind their husbands' backs, I have witnessed men do to their wives publicly with onlookers (including at church) as they scold or demean their wives. It is a dangerous habit to run down your spouse to others, whether privately or not. To do so privately is "gossip", which the Bible condemns. (e.g., Proverbs 18:8, 20:19, 26:20) People do this to find confirmation from others, and of course, the person telling the story is always the hero. To do so publicly (that is, to rebuke your spouse publicly in their presence) is typically abuse and/or manipulation, both of which demonstrate an unloving attitude.

If we are going to speak of our husband or wife to others, we should be able to do so with positive words. We should not run down our spouse to other people, including especially our friends and family. You may forgive them but those you gossiped to will not forgive and quite possibly will tell others. Throughout the Song, Solomon and Shulamite model a proper mindset about one another. Of course neither is perfect, but they measure one another by their good qualities and they articulate those qualities to one another in an encouraging way.

## Application Points

- **MAIN PRINCIPLE:** It is perfectly normal to have feelings of trepidation about the transition from single to married life, but for the right person, to consider their qualities is to be immediately reminded of their great value so that the apprehension is overcome.

- Your spouse should be in your eyes and your heart superior to all others and your speech should reflect that.

- Your significant other should be your best friend before being your lover.

## Discussion Questions

1. If you are married, what fears or anxieties did you have before marriage?

2. If you were to take Shulamite's approach and describe your significant other using only qualitative language, how would you describe them?

3. Is your qualitative description of your significant other different than when you first met? If not, why?

4. What is the difference between an acquaintance, a friend, and a best friend?

5. What does it say about a woman and her marriage if she feels the need to criticize her husband to others behind his back?

6. What does it say about a man and his marriage if he feels the need to publicly demean or scold his wife before other people?

7. Can you have a healthy marriage if your spouse is not your friend? What if they are not your best friend?

# Chapter 7

# Solomon in His Garden

In a world that uses phrases like "love at first sight," "falling in love" and "finding my soul mate," it is unsurprising that the meaning of love is ambiguous. The concept of loving a person and committing to them in marriage is described in terms more mystical than concrete, more emotional than rational, and more arbitrary than deliberate. But in the Bible, love is, in the first instance, a volitional commitment—with a beginning, without an end—to act in another's best interest. Such love does not occur by whim (love at first sight), accident (falling in love), or magic (finding my soul mate). Instead, it is built on selfless commitment. But a marriage also involves a strong emotional bond rooted in the deepest of friendships. A professor of mine always told us that people divorce for the same reason they get married. What he meant was that people verbally make the commitment of marriage because of what they believe they are getting and will continue to get from the relationship, but when they are no longer getting those benefits from the relationship, they either divorce or obtain those benefits from another through an affair.

This sort of selfish commitment is not love. The key is a selfless commitment, and to have a healthy, satisfying marriage, there must be mutual selfless commitment within a great friendship. This requires best friends who hold the same view about the love required to sustain a marriage and who are willing to make that mutual commitment.

## Scripture And Comments

In chapter 5 of the Song, Shulamite dreamed of rejecting Solomon's sexual advances and then searching for him. I suggested in the notes that the dream sequence represented the emotional turmoil Shulamite experienced ahead of the wedding as she contemplated growing up and transitioning from being one of the daughters of Jerusalem to being a married young woman. The chorus asked her in 5:9 what was so special about her Solomon that she would go searching for him, to which Shulamite explained the great qualities setting him apart from all other men. As the Song continues, the chorus responds to Shulamite, now willing to assist her in the search for Solomon.

DAUGHTERS

Song 6:1 Whither is thy beloved gone,

O thou fairest among women?

whither is thy beloved turned aside?

that we may seek him with thee.

After hearing Shulamite explain the unique and unsurpassed beauty of her Solomon, the daughters respond with the question, **whither is thy beloved gone, o**

**thou fairest among women? Whither is thy beloved turned aside?** Of course, Shulamite does not know, but the point of the questions is that Shulamite convinced the daughters that Solomon is worth searching for. This is why the daughters add, **that we may seek him with thee.** The chorus must acknowledge how exceptional Solomon is, well worth searching after.

> SHULAMITE
>
> 2 My beloved is gone down into his garden,
>
> to the beds of spices,
>
> to feed in the gardens,
>
> and to gather lilies.
>
> 3 I *am* my beloved's, and my beloved *is* mine:
>
> he feedeth among the lilies.

However, Shulamite does not need the daughters of Jerusalem to join her search for Solomon. She resolved the inner turmoil reflected in her dream and now welcomes her transition from the role of daughter to wife. Her **beloved** Solomon **is gone down into his garden**, a reference again to the sexual pleasures of her physical body (4:16). Any apprehension or fear is behind her and she is openly available to Solomon as she embraces the new season in her life. This is why she calls her body **his garden** instead of her garden. He has **gone...to the** garden **beds of spices.** Note that the phrase **bed of spices** is the same phrase Shulamite used to describe Solomon's cheeks (5:13). Rather than just something growing in the wild, her body is reflected as a designed or landscaped **bed of spices** where her lover may **feed in the gardens** and **gather lilies.** The point is that Solomon has free access to her body prepared for him so that he may be fully satisfied.

Their giving of one to the other physically is representative of their mutual commitment in their relationship. She summarizes their status: **I am my beloved's, and my beloved is mine: he feedeth among the lilies**. The phrase **he feedeth among the lilies** repeats what she said in 2:16, and indeed 2:16 and 6:3 are nearly identical. Solomon is fully sustained and satisfied in their mutual commitment of love. This mutual commitment to one another is a key ingredient to a healthy marriage. Men and women have many of the same emotional needs, but they do not, generally speaking, prioritize those needs in the same order. Men almost always see the need for sex as an expression of love as the number one need. Women usually see affection (apart from sex) as their top need. To have a mutual commitment where the relationship is fulfilling to both partners is to have a relationship where each is selflessly committed to understanding and meeting the needs of the other.

SOLOMON

4 Thou *art* beautiful, O my love, as Tirzah,

comely as Jerusalem,

terrible as *an army* with banners.

5 Turn away thine eyes from me,

for they have overcome me:

thy hair *is* as a flock of goats

that appear from Gilead.

6 Thy teeth *are* as a flock of sheep

which go up from the washing,

whereof every one beareth twins,

and *there is* not one barren among them.

7 As a piece of a pomegranate
*are* thy temples within thy locks.
8 There are threescore queens,
and fourscore concubines,
and virgins without number.
9 My dove, my undefiled is *but* one;
she *is* the *only* one of her mother,
she *is* the choice *one* of her that bare her.
The daughters saw her, and blessed her;
*yea*, the queens and the concubines, and they praised her.

With Shulamite's fears behind her and the marriage consummated, Solomon expresses in affectionate words his appreciation for her beauty. Just as Shulamite defended to the daughters her lover's qualities that make him better than all other men, so also Solomon will praise his Shulamite above all other women. This reciprocity provides unity to this portion of the Song (5:2-6:9).

Solomon exclaims that his Shulamite, his **love**, is **beautiful...as Tirzah, comely as Jerusalem, terrible as an army with banners**. The word **Tirzah** means, according to Strong's, "delightsomeness", or we might say "pleasure." Tirzah was a significant city (see, e.g., 1 Kings 15:33, 16:8) in northern Israel at the time of Solomon and only a short while thereafter, which is another indicator of an early date for the Song. And of course, Jerusalem is the key city in southern Israel or Judah, referenced in Lamentations 2:15 as "the perfection of beauty, the joy of the whole earth." Thus, Solomon compares her beauty to the choicest cities in the north and south. She is also as **terrible** or awesome **as an army with banners**. Similar imagery will be used again to describe her in 6:10. From a distance, an army in formation with its banners depicts strength and beauty. Indeed, so gorgeous is Shulamite that her beauty overwhelms her lover; he must ask her to **turn away thine eyes from me, for they have overcome me**. Just a glance of her eyes overtakes him. In the common English, Solomon might say as he sees her eyes, "mercy!" And framing her face is her **hair...as a flock of goats that appear from Gilead**, the familiar description of her locks that we saw in 4:1, describing the curls and movement of her long hair like the image of the herd of dark goats ascending or descending Mount **Gilead**.

The reader will notice that the description of her hair, teeth, and temples in 6:5-7 parallels the praise given her in 4:1-3. This, like the many other repetitions in the Song, affirms that it is best understood as a unified song and not a linear story or loosely related anthology. The beauty Solomon saw in Shulamite before the wedding night, he still sees in her after the wedding and consummation. Her **teeth are as a flock of sheep which go up from the washing**, meaning they are the purest white. Moreover, **every one beareth twins, and there is not one barren among them**. She has no missing or broken teeth. And **within** or behind her **locks** her **temples** are **as a piece of a pomegranate**. Solomon is not saying her **temples** physically resemble a **pomegranate**, but that her temples are sexually alluring. The imagery of the **pomegranate** occurs in 4:13 ("thy plants are an orchard of pomegranates, with pleasant fruits"), 6:11 ("...to see whether the vine flourished and the pomegranates budded"), 7:12 ("let us see if the vine flourish...and the pomegranates bud forth: there will I give thee my loves"), and 8:2 ("I would cause thee to drink of spiced wine of the juice of my pomegranate"). The **pomegranate** was considered an aphrodisiac in the ancient world, and through the Song is it used to convey a readiness (or ripeness) for lovemaking. And so here as well, his Shulamite is so lovely that even her **temples** are alluring.

This brings us to perhaps the most controversial verse in the Song. Solomon remarks that **there are threescore** (sixty) **queens, and fourscore** (eighty) **concubines, and virgins without number**. Expositors that attempt a fairly literal reading of the Song (i.e., that it describes a love affair and is not an allegory for God and Israel or Jesus and the Church) often see a necessity in defending the Song against this verse. They view the Song as extolling the idealism of Solomon's marriage to Shulamite, but this verse is seen as referencing Solomon's numerous other women. And thus, many fanciful interpretations are offered to maintain the literal historicity of the Solomon / Shulamite marriage and the idealism of their romance against the backdrop of Solomon's multitudes of lovers (e.g., that Shulamite was his first wife or the only one he really loved). Indeed, it is difficult to understand how the Song can extol the singular specialness of their relationship if Shulamite is just another lover in Solomon's harem.

Here again, keeping in the mind that the Song is poetry is key. First, the numbers here are not literal but used hypothetically for effect—there may be 60 **queens**, 80 **concubines**, numerous **virgins** (the daughters of Jerusalem), but Shulamite **my dove, my undefiled is but one** or is unique above all of them. Second, we must again emphasize that while Solomon wrote the Song and his persona serves as the male character in the Song, there is no reason to assume that the Song relates historical events, i.e., that he really married a woman named Shulamite and all of the dialogue in the Song really took place. And for this reason, there is no need to defend the Song. Solomon in many ways failed to live in accordance with God's standard despite his wisdom, yet his wisdom exceeded all others and was given to him by God. That he especially failed as concerning his many wives in no way detracts from the wisdom of the Song.

Solomon continues on the uniqueness of his Shulamite, **the only one of her mother**, likely meaning her only daughter. **She is the choice** or very best **of her that bare her** and so much so that even **the queens and the concubines...praised her**. This does not indicate that Shulamite is a member of the harem. Rather, the point is that those in the harem of the king are the beauty queens (the "Miss Jerusalem") of their day, and yet even they must acknowledge the exquisite beauty of Shulamite.

## Closing

As described in the book *His Needs, Her Needs* by Willard F. Harley, Jr., research has shown that men and women are wired differently when it comes to emotional needs, and especially with how they prioritize those needs. The core needs identified by Harley are admiration, affection, conversation, domestic support, family commitment, financial support, honesty and openness, physical attractiveness, recreational companionship, and sexual fulfillment. While not every man will prioritize his needs in the same order, and not every woman will prioritize her needs in the same order, almost all men will put sexual fulfillment first and almost all women will put affection (non-sexual) first. We can see in the passage considered in this chapter part of a pattern throughout the Song—sexual fulfillment and affection. For a man, sexual fulfillment and an intimate relationship with his wife are intertwined. Men need sex (they are biologically designed with high levels of testosterone), but what they truly want is not merely a willing partner but a responsive one. For women, affection (in words and non-sexual touching like hugs) and an intimate relationship are intertwined. Just like husbands do not want the humiliation of having to beg or manipulate their wives for sex, women do not want to have to ask for acts and words of affection. In the Song, we find Shulamite not only willing, but inviting and an initiator in their sexual pleasure. And while much of Solomon's words focus on Shulamite's physical appearance since the larger focus of the Song is physical romance, we clearly find Solomon to be a man who affectionately praises Shulamite in a way that extols her beauty but also her purity, strength, and uniqueness.

## <u>Application Points</u>

- **MAIN PRINCIPLE:** Marriage is founded on a selfless commitment to one another's needs.

- We should take notice of and verbalize our significant other's qualities.

- Primary needs include affection and sex and both should be met in a marriage.

## Discussion Questions

1. Why does the chorus seek to join in the search for Solomon?

2. Why does Shulamite in 6:2 refer to her body as "his garden"?

3. Do you want a spouse that permits you to have sex or do you want a responsive lover? Why does it matter?

4. What is the role of commitment in a friendship and a marriage?

5. Why is Solomon so head over heels for his wife? Is it just hormones or is there something more?

6. Is there a connection between Solomon's visit to the garden in 6:2, the commitment in 6:3, and his affectionate praise that follows?

# Chapter 8

# Shulamite Makes an Entrance

Our post-modern culture downplays the value of marriage. People are waiting longer to get married and still longer to have children. Our culture purports to exalt womanhood by tearing down the uniqueness of women in a race to eliminate gender differences under a banner of equality. The roles of mother and wife are secondary to education and career achievements. Yet the Bible exalts the roles of husband and wife and the enduring value of marriage as a unique God-ordained relationship. The Biblical role of the wife does not exclude education, employment, entrepreneurship or independence, but instead, the Bible paints a picture of a wife of tremendous dignity and value who is bright, industrious, takes initiative, and is independent and strong while prioritizing her duties to family. The world may see weakness in a woman who identifies with her role as a wife (and mother) as a first priority. But of this sort of wife, the Bible asks rhetorically: "Who can find a virtuous woman? for her price is far above rubies." (Proverbs 31:10)  Contrary to the caricature of the Biblical role of the wife as a sort of bondservant to her husband's selfish whims, she is presented as his greatest blessing among all human relationships, bringing completion to her husband and making him better. (Genesis 2:18)  In the transformation of Shulamite from daughter to wife, the Song presents Shulamite in her new role both beautiful and glorious.

## Scripture And Comments

Earlier in the Song, Solomon with his caravan "made an entrance" as they arrived to pick up Shulamite and escort her to the wedding, and the narrator announced his arrival to the daughters and to us.  Now it is Shulamite who is making the entrance with the narrator calling our attention to her glory.  Earlier in the Song, Shulamite remembered having some anxiety about the upcoming marriage as she contemplated the imminent life changes. She would leave behind forever the daughters of Jerusalem and that phase of her life to move forward as a married woman with new experiences and obligations. But none of this was to suggest that what lay ahead was not worth the exchange.  As we move through phases of life, good things are left behind us, but what God has for us next also presents blessings.  Having now experienced those blessings and embraced her new role, Shulamite is not less than what she was before, but more.  She is still beautiful Shulamite, but now as Solomon's wife, there is a new radiance about her.

NARRATOR

<u>Song 6:10</u> Who *is* she *that* looketh forth as the morning,

fair as the moon,

clear as the sun,

*and* terrible as *an army* with banners?

In response to Solomon's praise of the loveliness and uniqueness of his Shulamite, the narrator responds with a rhetorical question affirming Solomon's praise and serving as an announcement or heralding of the presence or arrival of the now married Shulamite. Recall that in 3:6 the narrator announced Solomon's arrival with a question. And later in 8:5, the narrator will announce the arrival or presence of the couple together. Thus, the pattern or touch points are that the narrator announced Solomon in his glory with his caravan, then newly married Shulamite in her radiance, and later the happy couple together. Within the Song, this is Shulamite's introduction to the audience as the now married Shulamite, previously of the daughters but now wife to Solomon. This verse begins the new unit of thought (6:10-8:7) presenting Shulamite embracing married life.

Of Shulamite, the narrator proclaims that **she...looketh forth as the morning** or the dawn, as **fair** or beautiful **as the moon**, as **clear** or bright **as the sun**, and as **terrible** or awe-inspiring **as an army with banners**. No woman can possibly compete with these accolades as Shulamite's beauty is on par with the Creator's greatest works, the sunrise, the **sun** and the **moon**. These manifestations of light in an unparalleled way capture the gaze of everyone. And by this means, the narrator affirms Solomon's assessment of her great uniqueness. The last phrase,

**terrible as an army with banners**, echoes Solomon's words emphasizing how awe-inspiring her presence is, just like the choreographed movements of an army with troops carrying their colored **banners**. But all of these words surpass even what was said earlier of Shulamite's beauty, and that is the point. Shulamite's beauty as a person is beyond physical attributes. She is radiant and stunning for Solomon (and as an example to the daughters and us) because of her commitment in her new role as his wife, and this gives her an additional quality she did not have before. As Solomon would say elsewhere, "Whoso findeth a wife findeth a good thing, and obtaineth favour of the LORD." (Proverbs 18:22) And as he said in Ecclesiastes 9:9: "Live joyfully with the wife whom thou lovest all the days of the life of thy vanity, which he [God] hath given thee under the sun...."

> SHULAMITE
>
> <u>11</u> I went down into the garden of nuts
>
> to see the fruits of the valley,
>
> *and* to see whether the vine flourished,
>
> *and* the pomegranates budded.
>
> <u>12</u> Or ever I was aware,
>
> my soul made me
>
> *like* the chariots of Amminadib.

With the formal introduction of the now married Shulamite having been made, Shulamite goes **down into the garden of nuts to see the fruits of the valley**. As with so much of the imagery in the Song, she is not really walking in a **garden** or inspecting **fruits**. Before she was waiting with great anticipation for Solomon to come to her, and then as she welcomed his presence, the marriage was consummated. Here, embracing her married life, she initiates lovemaking by inspecting for the abundance of the **garden** and the **valley**, to **see whether the vine flourished, and the pomegranates budded**. The emphasis in this imagery is that it is the season when there is abundance of sustaining **fruits, nuts, pomegranates**, etc., symbolizing sources of physical pleasures, from which she may partake. This speaks to Solomon's availability to her for lovemaking and her initiative and desire to partake of him. And her search for abundance in Solomon is satisfied so that she says **ever** or before **I was aware, my soul** or deepest inward desire **made me like the chariots of Amminadib**. The un-translated Hebrew term **Amminadib** means something like "my noble people" and probably does not refer to a place. Chariots are the tanks of the ancient world, in part because of their speed since they were drawn by horses. This simile likely conveys her arousal as a result of her trip to the **garden**, the **valley**, and by implication (from **whether the vine flourished**) the vineyard. Shulamite enjoys and embraces being Solomon's wife and lover.

DAUGHTERS

13 Return, return, O Shulamite;

return, return, that we may look upon thee.

To emphasize the fact that Shulamite is no longer a member of the daughters of Jerusalem but has now embraced and transitioned into her new role as wife to Solomon, the daughters call upon her to **return, return, O Shulamite; return, return, that we may look upon thee**. They want to stare at her, but she no longer belongs to them, must refuse their request, and must leave them behind.

SOLOMON

What will ye see in the Shulamite?

As it were the company of two armies.

Solomon responds to the daughters' plea for Shulamite's return so that they may gaze at her, asking, **what will ye see in the Shulamite?** His point is why should the daughters need to stare at her, and he adds, **as it were the company of two armies**. When **two armies** move toward or away from one another they have a semblance of being choreographed like a dance, akin to the movements of a modern marching band. The word **company** is the Hebrew *mchowiah*, which Strong's defines as "a dance:--company, dances(-cing)." The phrase **two armies** translates the Hebrew *mahanaim*, which Strong's defines as "an encampment (of travellers or troops); hence, an army, whether literal (of soldiers) or figurative (of dancers, angels, cattle, locusts, stars; or even the sacred courts):--army, band, battle, camp, company, drove, host, tents." Solomon is asking why the daughters would stare as **Shulamite** as if she were dancing like **two armies** or troops (perhaps of dancers). She is no longer a part of the daughters, but is his to gaze upon, which he will now do. His unusual question to the chorus transitions us to Shulamite's exotic private dance for Solomon.

SOLOMON

<u>Song 7:1</u> How beautiful are thy feet with shoes, O prince's daughter!

the joints of thy thighs *are* like jewels,

the work of the hands of a cunning workman.

<u>2</u> Thy navel *is like* a round goblet,

*which* wanteth not liquor:

thy belly *is like* an heap of wheat
set about with lilies.

3 Thy two breasts *are* like two young roes
*that are* twins.

4 Thy neck *is* as a tower of ivory;
thine eyes *like* the fishpools in Heshbon,
by the gate of Bathrabbim:
thy nose *is* as the tower of Lebanon
which looketh toward Damascus.

5 Thine head upon thee *is* like Carmel,
and the hair of thine head like purple;
the king *is* held in the galleries.

6 How fair and how pleasant art thou,
O love, for delights!

7 This thy stature is like to a palm tree,
and thy breasts to clusters *of grapes*.

8 I said, I will go up to the palm tree,
I will take hold of the boughs thereof:
now also thy breasts shall be as clusters of the
vine,
and the smell of thy nose like apples;

9 And the roof of thy mouth like the best wine

Solomon previously described and praised Shulamite's physical beauty (e.g., 4:1) beginning with her head and working down. But unlike before, here she is unclothed (except for sandals) and he starts at her feet and works his way up. Most likely, she is dancing for him, which fits contextually with Solomon's response to the daughters that alluded to her dancing and the fact that Solomon begins with her **feet** and **shoes**. The word **feet** translates the Hebrew *pa'am*, which Strong's defines as "a stroke, literally or figuratively (in various applications, as follow):--anvil, corner, foot(-step)...." Often the term is translated to indicate **feet** in motion, which fits here and explains why he bothers to mention her **shoes**. (e.g., Psalm 17:5, 57:6, 85:13, 119:133) Arnold Fruchtenbaum comments on this verse: "The Hebrew term translated 'feet' signifies *step and foot*, portraying her as dancing with her feet going back and forth."[1] Recalling that in this scene, Shulamite took the initiative in seeking to make love to Solomon, her erotic dance for him is in keeping with her taking the lead and seeking to arouse him.

Note that Solomon's description will mirror the sort of imagery Shulamite used of him (5:10-16) with the emphasis on craftsmanship. He notes **how beautiful** her **feet** are **with shoes** or sandals and calls her the **prince's** or nobleman's **daughter**, meaning noble or majestic qualities. Her **thighs are like jewels, the work of the hands of a cunning workman** or talented craftsman. Her **navel is like a round goblet, which wanteth not liquor**. In other words, Solomon likens the interior shape of her navel to a **goblet** or drinking glass (i.e., she is an "innie") that never runs dry, not suggesting literal drinking, but that her body is a continual source of (figuratively) intoxicating pleasure. Similarly, just as her body is figuratively an unending intoxicating drink, her **belly is** to be likened to endless food, **like an heap of wheat set about with lilies**. She is sexually his food and drink.

---

[1] Fruchtenbaum, Arnold G., *Biblical Lovemaking* (Tustin: Ariel Ministries Press, 2003), p. 55.

Continuing upward from her belly, Solomon next describes her **two breasts** as being **like two young roes that are twins**. This is almost exactly how he described her **breasts** in 4:5. Like prior poetic descriptions, he makes a visual comparison (e.g., flock of goats to her hair). The comparison here is two **young** gazelles identical in appearance standing near one another. These are not only beautiful and graceful animals, but they are **young** and full of life. By comparison, her **breasts** reflect the same youthful beauty and they satisfy him.

Solomon next moves to her **neck**, which **is as a tower of ivory**. This is similar to what Solomon said in 4:4: "Thy neck is like the tower of David builded for an armoury, whereon there hand a thousand bucklers, all shields of mighty men." The imagery of a **tower** conveys strength and perhaps that her neck has a pleasant length and symmetry to it. The imagery of **ivory** probably conveys the elegance of being crafted from the finest materials, and this is similar to Shulamite's earlier description of Solomon in terms of gold, gems and jewels, items that are finely crafted and artfully detailed by the great craftsman. Her **eyes** are **like the fishpools in Heshbon, by the gate of Bathrabbim**. The city of **Heshbon** was east of the northern portion of the Dead Sea, but archaeologists have not discovered the **gate of Bathrabbim** and so it is difficult to be dogmatic about the significance of this simile about her eyes. Implicitly, these must have been beautiful pools of some renown that caught the attention and gaze of those passing through the gate. Thus, what we can infer here is that Shulamite's eyes reflected a depth of beauty that was a particularly striking feature about her and gets the attention of others. As discussed in prior notes, this was the general concept behind

Solomon's compliment that she has dove's eyes (see notes on 4:1).

Shulamite's **nose** is **as the tower of Lebanon which looketh toward Damascus**. Up to this point, the Song has multiple times referred to **Lebanon**—the "wood of Lebanon" (3:9), "the smell of Lebanon" (4:11), "streams from Lebanon" (4:15), and "countenance as Lebanon" (5:15). **Lebanon** is the region north of Galilee bordering the Mediterranean, and **Damascus** is due east of **Lebanon**. Although we cannot be certain which **tower** is intended, like the prior comparison, we understand that he selected a familiar architectural marvel, and her **nose** is likewise an architectural marvel, which from a profile view points in a direction just like the **tower of Lebanon** was designed to point toward **Damascus**. Shulamite's **head** is **upon** her or crowns her **like** Mount **Carmel**, suggesting she is strong and tall. Her **hair** is **like purple**. Of course, this is a simile and the **purple** does not indicate the color of her **hair** but that her hair is like the royal curtains or tapestries, which traditionally were **purple**, finely crafted, lengthy and elegant. Recall that the upholstery in Solomon's coach was described as being **purple** (3:10). The beauty and length of her **hair** is such that **the king** could be **held** captive **in the galleries** or tresses of her **hair**. With the royal tapestries, a person might stand behind or wrapped within them as if captive, and by qualitative comparison, Shulamite's beautiful **hair** could figuratively take captive **the king** by commanding his gaze and perhaps the irresistibility of running his hands through her **hair**.

All of her beauty leads Solomon to conclude **how fair and how pleasant** she (his **love**) is **for delights**. We need not guess at what Solomon means by **delights** (or pleasures), for he quickly explains by likening her body **to a palm tree, and** her **breasts to clusters of grapes** that are ready to harvest. Solomon determines that he **will go up to the palm tree** and **take hold of the boughs** or branches with fruit on them. Her **breasts shall be as clusters** of grapes on **the vine** for Solomon's pleasure, **and the smell of** her **nose** or breath **like apples** as he kisses her. And as he kisses her, **the roof of** her **mouth** will be **like the best wine.** Obviously, her erotic dance had the desired effect of arousing Solomon. At this point, Shulamite will interrupt to complete Solomon's sentence and invite him to make love to her.

SHULAMITE

for my beloved, that goeth *down* sweetly,

causing the lips of those that are asleep to speak.

Finishing Solomon's sentence "the roof of thy mouth like the best wine", Shulamite says the wine is **for my beloved** Solomon, **that goeth down sweetly, causing the lips of those that are asleep to speak.** The **asleep** here is not literal sleeping (akin to how we might say "go to bed" and the intent is not to sleep). Rather, Shulamite's point is to invite his lovemaking by telling him that the wine will go **down sweetly** for both of them causing them to move their **lips** (continue kissing) as they lay together in bed. Thus, Shulamite is pictured as having embraced being Solomon's wife and lover, as demonstrated by her taking the initiative in their physical romance.

## Closing

The feminist caricature of women in the Bible is that they were simply oppressed chattels subject to their husbands' whims and abuses. While the ancient world and modern cultures have often been guilty of these charges, the Bible never condones such behavior. In reality, the Bible exalts womanhood in a way that was countercultural in the ancient world and largely remains so today. Shulamite is no servant, and her sexual relationship with Solomon is not just fulfilling obligations nor is she under duress. Instead, she is a spontaneous initiator. She is in every sense a lover, desiring her husband, seeking her own sexual pleasure from him, and seeking to please him. Shulamite is available, inviting, and physically responsive, and this is critical to the emotional needs of most men. Their marriage relationship reflects both passion and romance.

## Application Points

- **MAIN PRINCIPLE:** A married woman should embrace and prioritize her role and wife and lover, recognizing that God places a high value on the role of wife.

- Embracing the role of wife means that certain experiences that were a part of the blessing of being single must be abandoned or limited as the experiences and responsibilities of being a wife take priority. The same is true, by implication, for the husband.

- A wife should be willing to initiate in sexual pleasure and be available as a responsive lover.

- Sex within marriage is to be consensual and fulfilling for both the husband and wife.

## Discussion Questions

1. What is the significance of the narrator's introduction of Shulamite in 6:10?

2. What can we glean from verses like 6:11 that present Shulamite initiating the sexual experience?

3. As a wife leaves in the past her role as a daughter, what does that really look like? What sorts of experiences must be abandoned or limited as the role of wife is embraced?

4. How is Solomon's praise of Shulamite's beauty qualitatively different in 7:1-7 than in earlier descriptions?

5. Solomon expresses his strong desire in 7:8 to make love to his wife. As a marriage matures, should that desire remain, increase, go away, or change in some way?

6. What can a couple do to maintain the excitement of physical passion as the marriage matures?

# Chapter 9

# The City

In the book of Hebrews we read: "But now they desire a better country, that is, an heavenly: wherefore God is not ashamed to be called their God: for he hath prepared for them a city." (Hebrews 11:16) The verse captures the idea that faithful believers are pilgrims in this world looking for the heavenly country, the city God has prepared for them. While the context there has nothing to do with the subject of the Song, the beautiful language describing the blessing of the city that God has specially prepared for us could also describe the blessing God makes available to us in marriage. Jesus taught that God created marriage in the beginning and referred to marriage as that which "God hath joined." (Matthew 19:6) It is tremendously important that we not miss God's authorship of marriage and its blessings. Solomon in the book of Proverbs elaborated on the "city" available within a healthy marriage:

> Proverbs 5:15 Drink waters out of thine own cistern, and running waters out of thine own well. 16 Let thy fountains be

dispersed abroad, *and* rivers of waters in the streets. 17 Let them be only thine own, and not strangers' with thee. 18 Let thy fountain be blessed: and rejoice with the wife of thy youth.

To drink from "thine own cistern" and enjoy the "running waters out of thine own well" is for a man to take pleasure in the physical relationship he has with his wife. The married lovers enjoy their own private city where the "running waters" are uniquely and only theirs, a blessing that issues from the hand of God. It is a city of romance and a city of abundance, with "waters in the streets" where the lovers may "let [their] fountains be dispersed abroad." In this city, their "fountain" is "blessed" as the lovers "rejoice" together. In the Song, Shulamite and Solomon enjoy a prepared city, one of the unique private blessings they enjoy in abundance within the context of their marriage.

## Scripture And Comments

The passage analyzed in this chapter (Song 7:10-8:4) is part of the larger unit (6:10-8:4) of thought showing the marriage embraced and enjoyed by the lovers in their committed devotion to one another. Here, they explore their city and learn that the "running waters" need not run dry in a healthy marriage, but instead, the city yields new pleasures.

SHULAMITE

Song 7:10 I *am* my beloved's,
and his desire *is* toward me.

<u>11</u> Come, my beloved,

let us go forth into the field;

let us lodge in the villages.

<u>12</u> Let us get up early to the vineyards;

let us see if the vine flourish,

*whether* the tender grape appear,

*and* the pomegranates bud forth:

there will I give thee my loves.

<u>13</u> The mandrakes give a smell,

and at our gates *are* all manner of pleasant *fruits*,

new and old,

*which* I have laid up for thee, O my beloved.

Shulamite now confirms her satisfaction in wholly devoting herself to Solomon and embracing his physical desire for her: **I am my beloved's, and his desire is toward me**. Having willingly and joyously accepted her new role as Solomon's wife and the object of **his desire**, Shulamite now moves forward secure and satisfied in that new role, inviting him to take her on a trip to the countryside: **Come, my beloved, let us go forth into the field** or countryside and **lodge in the villages**. It will become apparent as the rest of the Song focuses on her mother's house and her brothers that this trip to the countryside is a trip to Shulamite's family home. It is a romantic trek where the lovers can **lodge in the villages** along the way and further enjoy one another.

Shulamite paints for Solomon a romantic and erotic invitation to entice him to this journey, and borrowing from the language in the introduction above, explore their city. Of course, that exploration is described in terms of a trip through the countryside. She suggests they can **rise early** in the morning **to go to the vineyards, to see if the** grape **vines flourish,** to see if **the tender grapes appear,** and **if the pomegranates bud forth.** Shulamite used nearly identical imagery in 6:11: "I went down into the garden of nuts to see the fruits of the valley, *and* to see whether the vine flourished, *and* the pomegranates budded." In both instances, the expressions do not mean a literal walk through the vineyard, but that she will initiate lovemaking in the early morning hours with Solomon to see if he is willing. This is clear from her conclusion—**there** in the vineyard **will I give thee my loves.** The term **loves** is the now familiar Hebrew *dod* by which is meant "lovemaking." In fact, in this figurative morning walk through the vineyard, **the mandrakes** (considered an aphrodisiac in the ancient world) **give a smell** and **at our gates are all manner of pleasant fruits, new and old, which I have laid up for thee, O my beloved.** As a married couple, their gardens mutually belong to one another and the gates do not exclude but welcome one another in. Shulamite tells Solomon she has stored up for him there **pleasant fruits, new and old.** She entices him erotically with the idea that their lovemaking will feature some things they have already experienced and some new experiences as well. This is the blessing of their city. We are not told explicitly what those **pleasant fruits** are nor does it matter. What is demonstrated is that in their married sex life there remains an excitement that is enhanced both by the idea of visiting a romantic location free of distractions and an energetic infusion of a little imagination within their gardens—their secret place for uninhibited mutual pleasure. This is surely the idea Solomon had in mind when he wrote to "let thy fountains be dispersed abroad, and rivers of water in the streets" of the city. The blessing of their physical union gets better and better, contrary to the often secular and cynical view of sex within a maturing marriage.

SHULAMITE

<u>Song 8:1</u> O that thou *wert* as my brother,

that sucked the breasts of my mother!

*when* I should find thee without,

I would kiss thee;

yea, I should not be despised.

<u>2</u> I would lead thee,

*and* bring thee into my mother's house, *who* would instruct me:

I would cause thee to drink of spiced wine

of the juice of my pomegranate.

<u>3</u> His left hand *should be* under my head,

and his right hand should embrace me.

<u>4</u> I charge you, O daughters of Jerusalem,

that ye stir not up, nor awake *my* love,

until he please.

Shulamite is excited about the sexual pleasures they will mutually enjoy, but she laments that they must be in private for her to physically express her affection for Solomon in any way. She even expresses hyperbole to make the point, wishing even **that** Solomon **wert as** her **brother, that sucked the breasts of** her **mother**. The reason she wishes he were like her **brother** is that she could **find** him **without** or outside in public, and as a brother she could **kiss** him in public and **not be despised** or reprimanded for violating a cultural taboo. Of course, her point is not that she would **kiss** her **brother** passionately, but that a public kiss to her **brother** would be socially permissible and she wishes she could **kiss** Solomon publicly and it likewise be socially permissible. But she wants to do more.

Recall that in the dream sequence of 3:1-4, prior to their wedding and during the time of boundaries and limitations in the courtship, Shulamite longed to bring Solomon "into my mother's house, and into the chamber of her that conceived me." (Song 3:4) While the complete meaning of this imagery is uncertain, Shulamite plainly finds significance in the notion of making love to him in the very bedroom where she was conceived. Now that she is married, she can disclose her secret desire to **lead** Solomon **into** her **mother's house** (and by implication to the room of her conception). Her mother is the one who **would instruct** Shulamite when she was a child living in that home. Now, Shulamite will give the instruction and **cause** Solomon **to drink of spiced wine of the juice of** her **pomegranate**, that is, to make love to her there.

Shulamite brings her erotic invitation to a close with the exact words she said in 2:6-7 where she invited Solomon to make love to her. She says, **his left hand should be under my head, and his right hand should embrace me**. This pictures the couple laying together in an embrace as they make love. Against the backdrop of Shulamite's secret sexual desire being disclosed and the reality that she and Solomon can now fully experience their mutual physical desires, she provides her third and final **charge** to the **daughters of Jerusalem, that** they **stir not up, nor awake *my* love, until he pleases**. As pointed out in earlier notes, the point here is not about waking Solomon, but waking their sexual desires before the proper time. In other words, the wonderful sexual experience (the city) the couple now has was the result of their waiting for the right person and the right time, and the **daughters** are told that if they want to have that blessing in their lives, they also must wait for the right person and right time before awaking sexual passions.

## Closing

I opened this chapter with a description of the city and how it is unique to each couple. With the beautiful poetry of Song 7:10-8:4 in mind, it is helpful to bring this chapter to a close with some further observations about the city. First, the city must have a population of two. In some marriages, there is only one (or none) and that is never healthy. For the city to function it requires two, each seeking to provide what pleases the other. This requires communications and likely some experimentation as the lovers learn what pleases one another. Second, and corollary to the first, the city does not function if the sexual pleasures are not mutual. If the experience is not mutually consented to, it should not occur.

Third, the city must be explored for the waters to run through the streets (it is the lovers in their lovemaking running through the streets of their personal city). This means that a mutual willingness to experiment and explore (and not do exactly the same thing every time you make love) will be part of the blessing. Fourth, Shulamite talked about lodging in the villages. There is much to be said about how lovers must be deliberate in cultivating their city. In our busy lives there are many distractions that can make physical romance a race rather than a rhythm and a routine rather than a rediscovery. The enduring pleasures the Song assures us can be ours do not occur by accident. With busy schedules and especially with children, times and sometimes locations need to be deliberately set aside for some planned spontaneity. Finally, there can never be three in the city. Affairs within marriage are extraordinarily common and it is beyond the scope here to address that in any detail. But at the core, when a spouse has long-term unmet needs within the marriage, they are at a high risk of inviting someone outside the marriage to fill those needs (and this is absolutely not limited to unmet sexual needs). An affair does not develop overnight and most cheaters feel guilty about their conduct and explain that it "just happened". Invariably the affair begins with someone outside the marriage meeting a need the spouse does not meet, and before long they are invited into the city. Affair proof marriages involve both spouses consciously seeking to understand their partner's needs and meeting them.

## Application Points

- **MAIN PRINCIPLE:** The blessing within marriage of physical romance is intended to be an enduring source of pleasure.

## Discussion Questions

1. If the sexual aspects of your marriage constitute your unique "city," what steps can you take so that the waters continue to run through the streets even after several years of marriage?

2.  In what ways might a literal trip (without children) and lodging in the villages along the way enhance the sexual experience within the marriage?

3.  What do you think Shulamite means when she says she will show Solomon "pleasant fruits, new and old" that she has "laid up for" him?

4.  What are some ways you can store away some things "new and old" for a romantic rendezvous?

5.  What is pornography?  Is viewing pornography wrong and, if so, why?

6.  How does viewing pornography impact the spouse viewing it?  The other spouse?  The children?

# Chapter 10

# The Couple Makes an Entrance

The world is changing rapidly and almost all of it is entirely beyond our control. Even for those who embrace change, there is a core need to have some constants in our universe. Of course, the Bible affirms that with God there is "no variableness, neither shadow of turning." (James 1:17) But the other relationship where we can find some constants that we need is in our marriage. In this world that changes so quickly, we must always be for our spouse a fixed point of comfort, encouragement, hope, love and strength in each other's lives. As the Song comes to a close, God affirms to us not only the permanency of marriage, but the enduring strength of love within a marriage that is designed to be a reliable constant. It is the knowledge that you are loved and will continue to be loved that creates a safe haven relationship where your total person can be revealed and not concealed, liberating husband and wife to live and learn and love and grow as they run hand in hand down their path of life together. And this experience, the Song reminds us, cannot be purchased.

## Scripture And Comments

We previously witnessed the narrator announcing the entrance of Solomon's caravan (Song 3:6-11) and the newly married Shulamite (Song 6:10). Now, as the Song closes, it does so with the narrator announcing the entrance of the married couple. Just as Solomon's caravan arrived "out of the wilderness" from its journey, so also now the happy couple will arrive from their journey through the wilderness. We have the privilege of witnessing their arrival and rejoicing in God's blessing on their marriage.

> NARRATOR
>
> Song 8:5 Who *is* this that cometh up from the wilderness,
>
> leaning upon her beloved?

This is the narrator's third and final introduction. In 3:6 he introduced (in the form of a question) Solomon with his wedding caravan: "Who is this that cometh out of the wilderness like pillars of smoke, perfumed with myrrh and frankincense, with all powders of the merchant?" Then in 6:10, the narrator introduced the newly married Shulamite with all of her wedding day fears behind her and her new life with Solomon embraced: "Who is she that looketh forth as the morning, fair as the moon, clear as the sun, and terrible as an army with banners?" And now the narrator introduces the happy couple together, viewed as approaching from the wilderness the way Solomon approached with his caravan to receive Shulamite and escort her to the wedding. As already noted, their trip to the countryside would seem to be a trip to her family home, thus bringing much of the "story" underlying the Song full circle. This would make sense of the similar announcement from the narrator about their approach **from the wilderness**. The reference to **cometh up** suggests they are approaching mountains and traveling to higher elevations. Shulamite is **leaning upon her beloved** Solomon as they approach.

> SHULAMITE
> I raised thee up under the apple tree:
> there thy mother brought thee forth:
> there she brought thee forth *that* bare thee.
> 6 Set me as a seal upon thine heart,
> as a seal upon thine arm:
> for love *is* strong as death;
> jealousy *is* cruel as the grave:
> the coals thereof *are* coals of fire,
> *which hath a* most vehement flame.
> 7 Many waters cannot quench love,
> neither can the floods drown it:
> if *a* man would give all the substance of his house for love,
> it would utterly be contemned.

Upon the couple being introduced by the narrator, Shulamite addresses Solomon. The Song previously referenced a tree or trees six times. In particular, Solomon was an "apple tree" (2:3), the "fig tree" was fruitful (2:13), there were "trees of frankincense" (4:14), and Shulamite was like a "palm tree" (7:7-8). Shulamite now says that she **raised** Solomon **up under the apple**

**tree**. The term **raised** translates the Hebrew *oor*, which Strong's defines as follows: "to wake (literally or figuratively...raise (up), stir up (self)." The context makes plain that she did not literally "wake" Solomon **under the apple tree**, but figuratively **raised** or stirred him, meaning aroused him sexually in the location where Solomon's **mother brought** him **forth: there she brought** Solomon **forth that bare thee**. Recall that in one of the dream sequences Shulamite stated: "*It was* but a little that I passed from them, but I found him whom my soul loveth: I held him, and would not let him go, <u>until I had brought him into my mother's house, and into the chamber of her that conceived me</u>." (Song 3:4) While the precise reason is unknown, Shulamite obviously places great significance upon making love to Solomon in the place where she was conceived. Here in 8:5, she reflects on arousing Solomon—and by implication making love to him—in the place where he was conceived and born. Note the parallels in the two passages, although the motifs in chapter 8 are presented in a different order (compare 3:4 to second half of 8:5, 3:5 to 8:4, 3:6 to first half of 8:5).

Shulamite now calls upon Solomon to **set me as a seal upon thine heart** and **as a seal upon thine arm**. A signet or **seal** was an engraved stone used to show ownership by stamping an impression on soft clay or wax. The stone was worn on a necklace or bracelet and was so valuable that the owner would always wear it or have it near at hand. Thus, what Shulamite expresses here is her desire to be like Solomon's signet, an object practically identified with its owner. We especially see here that while the Song may be misunderstood as primarily focused on sex, the sexual pleasures they enjoy display the quality of their **love**, their bond and the intimacy between them. Shulamite here expresses her desire for that quality of intimacy that is present in marriages where husband and wife are nearly inseparable, a quality that is not just about sex but proximity of the hearts, commitment, friendship, trust, and having a safe place relationship.

As Shulamite reflects on her relationship with Solomon and against the backdrop imagery of the inseparability of the **seal** from its owner, she concludes that **love is as strong as death**. Of course, **death** is both permanent and irresistible. In like manner, **jealousy is cruel** or severe **as the grave**. The term *qinah* translated **jealousy** does not here denote the negative emotion that occurs when we fear someone taking something we have. Rather, it can denote the positive side of love in action, and can be translated as "zeal" or passion (2 Kings 10:16, 19:31, Psalm 119:139). Her point is that **love** generates passion or zeal that is unrelenting **as the grave**, which of course never lets go of the one in its grasp. These words speak of the permanency of the **love** that unites them in marriage, but more than that, their **love** is zealous and unrelenting toward one another. Moreover, their loves is all consuming of their relationship, for **the coals thereof are coals of fire, which hath a most vehement flame**.

The consuming fire of the sort of **love** shared by Shulamite and Solomon cannot be doused, for **many waters cannot quench love**. Even **the floods** cannot **drown** out love. More than that, you cannot buy this love. For **if a man would give all the substance of his house** (all his wealth) **for love, it would be utterly be contemned** or despised. Relative to the great value of this sort of **love**, possessions and wealth are of such little value as to be altogether despised.

BROTHERS

<u>8</u> We have a little sister,

and she hath no breasts:

what shall we do for our sister

in the day when she shall be spoken for?

<u>9</u> If she *be* a wall,

we will build upon her a palace of silver:

and if she *be* a door,

we will inclose her with boards of cedar.

Recall that in the first chapter, Shulamite expressed anger at her brothers for making her work in the family vineyard because her daily exposure to the sun caused her body to be darkly tanned: "Look not upon me, because I *am* black, because the sun hath looked upon me: my mother's children were angry with me; they made me the keeper of the vineyards; *but* mine own vineyard have I not kept." (Song 1:6) The present passage will bring closure to this issue by first reflecting back on the decision that led to Shulamite's brothers making her work the vineyards. Shulamite recalls their decision. Her brothers reasoned that **we have a little sister, and she hath no breasts**. This refers to Shulamite, likely as a pre-teen. They know she will soon be going through puberty and they want to protect her purity.

Her brothers ask the question, **what shall we do for our sister in the day when she shall be spoken for?** In other words, they seek to do something in her best interest for her future marriage (**when she shall be spoken for**). They reason that **if she be a wall, we will build upon her a palace of silver**. In other words, if Shulamite shows herself virtuous (**a wall** protects a city; here she is **a wall** protecting her own purity), then her brothers will add on to the **wall** (i.e., Shulamite) **a palace of silver**. They will add to Shulamite's own fortification of her purity, but in a positive way. On the other hand, **if she be a door**, suggesting a young lady who cares little for her purity and virtue, her brothers **will inclose her with boards of cedar**. In other words, her brothers will take great lengths to protect her purity even if that requires negative actions, which likely include restrictions.

SHULAMITE

10 I *am* a wall,

and my breasts like towers:

then was I in his eyes

as one that found favour.

11 Solomon had a vineyard at Baalhamon;

he let out the vineyard unto keepers;

every one for the fruit thereof was to bring

a thousand *pieces* of silver.

12 My vineyard, which *is* mine, *is* before me:

thou, O Solomon, *must have* a thousand,

and those that keep the fruit thereof two hundred.

Assessing her memory of what her brothers did to protect her purity, Shulamite affirms that she is **a wall, and** her **breasts like towers**. Thanks to her brothers' efforts, she was **a wall**, protective of her sexual purity. She is no longer the "little sister...[with] no breasts" but fully grown with the breasts of a woman and not a child. Because of her beauty and purity, she was **in his** (Solomon's) **eyes as one that found favour**. Shulamite now recounts how she came to be **in his eyes**, namely that Solomon owned **a vineyard at Baalhamon**, the exact location of which is unknown. Solomon **let out** or leased **the vineyard unto keepers**, meaning those who would maintain the **vineyard** to produce its fruit. The rental price **for the fruit thereof** was **a thousand pieces of silver**. Since we know from 1:6 that her family maintained a **vineyard**, a reasonable inference is that Shulamite's family rented Solomon's **vineyard at Baalhamon**. Again, whether or not the Song intends to convey historical events, or instead the backstory of the Song is essentially fictional and serves only as a device to relay wisdom, may be debated, but in either event the wisdom (the message) is the same.

In contrast to Solomon's literal **vineyard** that is shared with those who rent it, Shulamite's figurative **vineyard, which is** hers, **is before** her. Recall that this play on words comparing the literal **vineyard** to the figurative **vineyard** of Shulamite's body occurred in 1:6, and in several other places the Song refers to vineyards (1:14, 2:15, 7:12). She notes that the rent money (**a thousand** shekels) goes to Solomon and **two hundred** shekels goes to **those that keep** or maintain **the fruit thereof**, namely her brothers. But now that she is no longer a child under her brothers' care, unlike the literal **vineyard**, her **vineyard** (physical body) is wholly her own to maintain and to share the fruit as she sees fit.

SOLOMON

13 Thou that dwellest in the gardens,

the companions hearken to thy voice:
cause me to hear *it.*

The Song comes to a close much as it opened, with an invitation. (Song 1:4) Solomon calls to her **that dwellest in the gardens** and advises her that **the companions hearken to** hear her **voice**, and he asks that she **cause** him **to hear** her voice. The **companions** may refer to their friends who want to hear her, or perhaps is a device to refer to the audience or hearer of the Song who would hear form Shulamite—the clear "lead" in the Song—one last time as it comes to a close. Recall that in 2:14, Solomon asked to hear her voice: "let me hear they voice; for sweet is they voice, and thy countenance is comely." He made that invitation to her in the context of their separation (she was "in the clefts of the rock"). Here also, they are separated (not because of the boundaries present during their courtship) and Solomon longs **to hear** her voice.

SHULAMITE
<u>14</u> Make haste, my beloved,
and be thou like to a roe
or to a young hart
upon the mountains of spices.

In response to Solomon's invitation, Shulamite invites him to **make haste, my beloved, and be thou like to a roe** or gazelle **or to a young heart** or stag **upon the mountains of spices**. The Song previously used "mountain" or "mountains" as metaphors for Shulamite's breasts. (Song 2:17, 4:6) And likewise here, the **mountains of spices** refers to her breasts. Thus, the Song closes with Shulamite's invitation to Solomon to make love to her.

## Closing

As I have tried to maintain through the book, the Song is not really a story even though it has limited elements of a story. Instead, it is throughout a song whose goal is to describe emotions, passions and states of the lovers so that we may understand them and hear their words against the backdrop of the love and romance they share with one another. Stories lead to endings, but the Song has no ending as such. Rather, the Song invites us into a small slice of Shulamite's and Solomon's world, and ultimately their "city" as I used the term previously. We were permitted to see through their eyes, hear their words, and experience their emotions, including especially their longing to be together as husband and wife and to physically express their love. The Song began with desire and longing for the day of their union. The Song finishes with the desire and longing in a state of continuing satisfaction. But the Song takes us beyond merely the physical side of their lovemaking. The passion and satisfaction they have and will continue to enjoy is emblematic of their committed love and the intimacy of their relationship. The Song was a journey to this place, this city, this status of being that is theirs for as long as they live. The basic wisdom of the book—to reserve sexual pleasures for the right person in the context of marriage—is widely rejected today, yet nearly everyone wants what Shulamite and Solomon had. Like all pages of the Bible, the Song puts the verdict (the "how now shall I live?") in our hands. It is not enough to want what they had. The Song invites the reader to align their thinking with God by faith in order to experience the very best He has for them in marriage.

## Application Points

- **MAIN PRINCIPLE:** A mutually satisfying sexual relationship within a marriage is an outpouring of the commitment, intimacy and love within the marriage.

- It is appropriate within our sphere of influence to be protective of the sexual purity of others.

## Discussion Questions

1. What is the significance of the narrator's introduction?

2. What is (non-physical) intimacy within a marriage? How can it be created and sustained?

3. In practical terms, what does a marriage look like with / without (non-physical) intimacy?

4. Shulamite speaks eloquently of the power of love in 8:6-7, but what is love as she uses the term?

5. Why do you think the Song ends the way it does?

# Appendix

# The Song of Solomon

<u>Song 1:1</u> The song of songs, which *is* Solomon's.

SHULAMITE

<u>Song 1:2</u> Let him kiss me with the kisses of his
mouth:
for thy love *is* better than wine.
3 Because of the savour of thy good ointments
thy name *is as* ointment poured forth,
therefore do the virgins love thee.
4 Draw me, we will run after thee:
the king hath brought me into his chambers:

DAUGHTERS

we will be glad and rejoice in thee,
we will remember thy love more than wine:

SHULAMITE

    the upright love thee.
    5 I *am* black, but comely,
    O ye daughters of Jerusalem,
    as the tents of Kedar,
    as the curtains of Solomon.
    6 Look not upon me, because I *am* black,
    because the sun hath looked upon me:
    my mother's children were angry with me;
    they made me the keeper of the vineyards;
    *but* mine own vineyard have I not kept.
    7 Tell me, O thou whom my soul loveth,
    where thou feedest,
    where thou makest *thy flock* to rest at noon:
    for why should I be as one that turneth aside
    by the flocks of thy companions?

DAUGHTERS

    8 If thou know not,
    O thou fairest among women,
    go thy way forth by the footsteps of the flock,
    and feed thy kids beside the shepherds' tents.

SOLOMON

    9 I have compared thee, O my love,
    to a company of horses in Pharaoh's chariots.
    10 Thy cheeks are comely with rows *of jewels*,
    thy neck with chains *of gold*.
    11 We will make thee borders of gold
    with studs of silver.

## SHULAMITE

12 While the king *sitteth* at his table,
my spikenard sendeth forth the smell thereof.
13 A bundle of myrrh *is* my wellbeloved unto me;
he shall lie all night betwixt my breasts.
14 My beloved *is* unto me *as* a cluster of camphire
in the vineyards of Engedi.

## SOLOMON

15 Behold, thou *art* fair, my love;
behold, thou *art* fair;
thou *hast* doves' eyes.

## SHULAMITE

16 Behold, thou *art* fair, my beloved,
yea, pleasant:
also our bed *is* green.
17 The beams of our house *are* cedar,
*and* our rafters of fir.

## SHULAMITE

Song 2:1 I *am* the rose of Sharon,
*and* the lily of the valleys.

## SOLOMON

2 As the lily among thorns,
so *is* my love among the daughters.

## SHULAMITE

3 As the apple tree among the trees of the wood,
so *is* my beloved among the sons.
I sat down under his shadow with great delight,
and his fruit *was* sweet to my taste.
4 He brought me to the banqueting house,
and his banner over me *was* love.
5 Stay me with flagons,
comfort me with apples:
for I *am* sick of love.
6 His left hand *is* under my head,
and his right hand doth embrace me.
7 I charge you, O ye daughters of Jerusalem,
by the roes, and by the hinds of the field,
that ye stir not up, nor awake *my* love,
till he please.
8 The voice of my beloved!
behold, he cometh leaping upon the mountains,
skipping upon the hills.
9 My beloved is like a roe
or a young hart:
behold, he standeth behind our wall,
he looketh forth at the windows,
shewing himself through the lattice.
10 My beloved spake, and said unto me,

## SOLOMON

Rise up, my love,
my fair one, and come away.
11 For, lo, the winter is past,
the rain is over *and* gone;

12 The flowers appear on the earth;
the time of the singing *of birds* is come,
and the voice of the turtle is heard in our land;
13 The fig tree putteth forth her green figs,
and the vines *with* the tender grape give a *good* smell.
Arise, my love,
my fair one, and come away.
14 O my dove, *that art* in the clefts of the rock,
in the secret *places* of the stairs,
let me see thy countenance,
let me hear thy voice;
for sweet *is* thy voice,
and thy countenance *is* comely.

SHULAMITE

15 Take us the foxes,
the little foxes, that spoil the vines:
for our vines *have* tender grapes.
16 My beloved *is* mine, and I *am* his:
he feedeth among the lilies.
17 Until the day break,
and the shadows flee away,
turn, my beloved, and be thou like a roe
or a young hart upon the mountains of Bether.
Song 3:1 By night on my bed
I sought him whom my soul loveth:
I sought him, but I found him not.
2 I will rise now, and go about the city
in the streets, and in the broad ways
I will seek him whom my soul loveth:
I sought him, but I found him not.

3 The watchmen that go about the city found me:
*to whom I said,* Saw ye him whom my soul loveth?
4 *It was* but a little that I passed from them,
but I found him whom my soul loveth:
I held him, and would not let him go,
until I had brought him into my mother's house,
and into the chamber of her that conceived me.
5 I charge you, O ye daughters of Jerusalem,
by the roes, and by the hinds of the field,
that ye stir not up, nor awake *my* love,
till he please.

## NARRATOR

6 Who *is* this that cometh out of the wilderness
like pillars of smoke,
perfumed with myrrh and frankincense,
with all powders of the merchant?
7 Behold his bed, which *is* Solomon's;
threescore valiant men *are* about it,
of the valiant of Israel.
8 They all hold swords,
*being* expert in war:
every man *hath* his sword upon his thigh
because of fear in the night.
9 King Solomon made himself a chariot
of the wood of Lebanon.
10 He made the pillars thereof *of* silver,
the bottom thereof *of* gold,
the covering of it *of* purple,
the midst thereof being paved *with* love,
for the daughters of Jerusalem.
11 Go forth, O ye daughters of Zion,

and behold king Solomon
with the crown wherewith his mother crowned
him
in the day of his espousals,
and in the day of the gladness of his heart.

## SOLOMON

<u>Song 4:1</u> Behold, thou *art* fair, my love;
behold, thou *art* fair;
thou *hast* doves' eyes within thy locks:
thy hair *is* as a flock of goats,
that appear from mount Gilead.
<u>2</u> Thy teeth *are* like a flock *of sheep that are even*
shorn,
which came up from the washing;
whereof every one bear twins,
and none *is* barren among them.
3 Thy lips *are* like a thread of scarlet,
and thy speech *is* comely:
thy temples *are* like a piece of a pomegranate
within thy locks.
<u>4</u> Thy neck *is* like the tower of David
builded for an armoury, whereon there hang
a thousand bucklers,
all shields of mighty men.
<u>5</u> Thy two breasts *are* like two young roes
that are twins, which feed among the lilies.
<u>6</u> Until the day break,
and the shadows flee away,
I will get me to the mountain of myrrh,
and to the hill of frankincense.
<u>7</u> Thou *art* all fair, my love;

*there is* no spot in thee.

<u>8</u> Come with me from Lebanon, *my* spouse,
with me from Lebanon:
look from the top of Amana,
from the top of Shenir and Hermon,
from the lions' dens,
from the mountains of the leopards.

<u>9</u> Thou hast ravished my heart, my sister, *my* spouse;
thou hast ravished my heart with one of thine eyes,
with one chain of thy neck.

<u>10</u> How fair is thy love, my sister, *my* spouse!
how much better is thy love than wine!
and the smell of thine ointments than all spices!

<u>11</u> Thy lips, O *my* spouse, drop *as* the honeycomb:
honey and milk *are* under thy tongue;
and the smell of thy garments *is* like the smell of Lebanon.

<u>12</u> A garden inclosed *is* my sister, *my* spouse;
a spring shut up, a fountain sealed.

<u>13</u> Thy plants *are* an orchard of pomegranates,
with pleasant fruits;
camphire, with spikenard,

<u>14</u> Spikenard and saffron; calamus and cinnamon,
with all trees of frankincense;
myrrh and aloes,
with all the chief spices:

<u>15</u> A fountain of gardens,
a well of living waters,
and streams from Lebanon.

## SHULAMITE

<u>16</u> Awake, O north wind;
and come, thou south;
blow upon my garden,
*that* the spices thereof may flow out.
Let my beloved come into his garden,
and eat his pleasant fruits.

## SOLOMON

<u>Song 5:1</u> I am come into my garden, my sister, *my*
spouse:
I have gathered my myrrh with my spice;
I have eaten my honeycomb with my honey;
I have drunk my wine with my milk:

## NARRATOR

eat, O friends;
drink, yea, drink abundantly, O beloved.

## SHULAMITE

<u>2</u> I sleep, but my heart waketh:
*it is* the voice of my beloved that knocketh,
*saying*,

## SOLOMON

Open to me, my sister, my love,
my dove, my undefiled:
for my head is filled with dew,

*and* my locks with the drops of the night.
SHULAMITE

3 I have put off my coat;
how shall I put it on?
I have washed my feet;
how shall I defile them?
4 My beloved put in his hand by the hole *of the door*,
and my bowels were moved for him.
5 I rose up to open to my beloved;
and my hands dropped *with* myrrh,
and my fingers *with* sweet smelling myrrh,
upon the handles of the lock.
6 I opened to my beloved;
but my beloved had withdrawn himself, *and* was gone:
my soul failed when he spake:
I sought him, but I could not find him;
I called him, but he gave me no answer.
7 The watchmen that went about the city found me,
 they smote me, they wounded me;
the keepers of the walls
took away my veil from me.
8 I charge you, O daughters of Jerusalem,
if ye find my beloved,
that ye tell him, that I *am* sick of love.

DAUGHTERS

9 What *is* thy beloved more than *another* beloved,
O thou fairest among women?
what *is* thy beloved more than *another* beloved,

that thou dost so charge us?
SHULAMITE

10 My beloved *is* white and ruddy,
the chiefest among ten thousand.
11 His head *is as* the most fine gold,
his locks *are* bushy, *and* black as a raven.
12 His eyes *are* as *the eyes* of doves
by the rivers of waters,
washed with milk,
*and* fitly set.
13 His cheeks *are* as a bed of spices,
*as* sweet flowers:
his lips *like* lilies,
dropping sweet smelling myrrh.
14 His hands *are as* gold rings
set with the beryl:
his belly *is as* bright ivory
overlaid *with* sapphires.
15 His legs *are as* pillars of marble,
set upon sockets of fine gold:
his countenance *is* as Lebanon,
excellent as the cedars.
16 His mouth *is* most sweet:
yea, he *is* altogether lovely.
This *is* my beloved, and this *is* my friend,
O daughters of Jerusalem.

DAUGHTERS

Song 6:1 Whither is thy beloved gone,
O thou fairest among women?
whither is thy beloved turned aside?

that we may seek him with thee.

SHULAMITE

2 My beloved is gone down into his garden,
to the beds of spices,
to feed in the gardens,
and to gather lilies.
3 I *am* my beloved's, and my beloved *is* mine:
he feedeth among the lilies.

SOLOMON

4 Thou *art* beautiful, O my love, as Tirzah,
comely as Jerusalem,
terrible as *an army* with banners.
5 Turn away thine eyes from me,
for they have overcome me:
thy hair *is* as a flock of goats
that appear from Gilead.
6 Thy teeth *are* as a flock of sheep
which go up from the washing,
whereof every one beareth twins,
and *there is* not one barren among them.
7 As a piece of a pomegranate
*are* thy temples within thy locks.
8 There are threescore queens,
and fourscore concubines,
and virgins without number.
9 My dove, my undefiled is *but* one;
she *is* the *only* one of her mother,
she *is* the choice *one* of her that bare her.
The daughters saw her, and blessed her;

*yea*, the queens and the concubines, and they
praised her.

NARRATOR

<u>10</u> Who *is* she *that* looketh forth as the morning,
fair as the moon,
clear as the sun,
*and* terrible as *an army* with banners?

SHULAMITE

<u>11</u> I went down into the garden of nuts
to see the fruits of the valley,
*and* to see whether the vine flourished,
*and* the pomegranates budded.
<u>12</u> Or ever I was aware,
my soul made me
*like* the chariots of Amminadib.

DAUGHTERS

<u>13</u> Return, return, O Shulamite;
return, return, that we may look upon thee.

SOLOMON

What will ye see in the Shulamite?
As it were the company of two armies.
<u>Song 7:1</u> How beautiful are thy feet with shoes, O
prince's daughter!
the joints of thy thighs *are* like jewels,
the work of the hands of a cunning workman.
<u>2</u> Thy navel *is like* a round goblet,

*which* wanteth not liquor:
thy belly *is like* an heap of wheat
set about with lilies.
3 Thy two breasts *are* like two young roes
*that are* twins.
4 Thy neck *is* as a tower of ivory;
thine eyes *like* the fishpools in Heshbon,
by the gate of Bathrabbim:
thy nose *is* as the tower of Lebanon
which looketh toward Damascus.
5 Thine head upon thee *is* like Carmel,
and the hair of thine head like purple;
the king *is* held in the galleries.
6 How fair and how pleasant art thou,
O love, for delights!
7 This thy stature is like to a palm tree,
and thy breasts to clusters *of grapes*.
8 I said, I will go up to the palm tree,
I will take hold of the boughs thereof:
now also thy breasts shall be as clusters of the vine,
and the smell of thy nose like apples;
9 And the roof of thy mouth like the best wine

SHULAMITE

for my beloved, that goeth *down* sweetly,
causing the lips of those that are asleep to speak.
10 I *am* my beloved's,
and his desire *is* toward me.
11 Come, my beloved,
let us go forth into the field;
let us lodge in the villages.

12 Let us get up early to the vineyards;
let us see if the vine flourish,
*whether* the tender grape appear,
*and* the pomegranates bud forth:
there will I give thee my loves.
13 The mandrakes give a smell,
and at our gates *are* all manner of pleasant *fruits*,
new and old,
*which* I have laid up for thee, O my beloved.
Song 8:1 O that thou *wert* as my brother,
that sucked the breasts of my mother!
*when* I should find thee without,
I would kiss thee;
yea, I should not be despised.
2 I would lead thee,
*and* bring thee into my mother's house, *who*
would instruct me:
I would cause thee to drink of spiced wine
of the juice of my pomegranate.
3 His left hand *should be* under my head,
and his right hand should embrace me.
4 I charge you, O daughters of Jerusalem,
that ye stir not up, nor awake *my* love,
until he please.

NARRATOR

5 Who *is* this that cometh up from the wilderness,
leaning upon her beloved?

SHULAMITE

I raised thee up under the apple tree:

there thy mother brought thee forth:
there she brought thee forth *that* bare thee.
6 Set me as a seal upon thine heart,
as a seal upon thine arm:
for love *is* strong as death;
jealousy *is* cruel as the grave:
the coals thereof *are* coals of fire,
*which hath a* most vehement flame.
7 Many waters cannot quench love,
neither can the floods drown it:
if *a* man would give all the substance of his house for love,
it would utterly be contemned.

## BROTHERS

8 We have a little sister,
and she hath no breasts:
what shall we do for our sister
in the day when she shall be spoken for?
9 If she *be* a wall,
we will build upon her a palace of silver:
and if she *be* a door,
we will inclose her with boards of cedar.

## SHULAMITE

10 I *am* a wall,
and my breasts like towers:
then was I in his eyes
as one that found favour.
11 Solomon had a vineyard at Baalhamon;
he let out the vineyard unto keepers;

every one for the fruit thereof was to bring
a thousand *pieces* of silver.
12 My vineyard, which *is* mine, *is* before me:
thou, O Solomon, *must have* a thousand,
and those that keep the fruit thereof two
hundred.

SOLOMON

13 Thou that dwellest in the gardens,
the companions hearken to thy voice:
cause me to hear *it*.

SHULAMITE

14 Make haste, my beloved,
and be thou like to a roe
or to a young hart
upon the mountains of spices.

# Bibliography

Barry, J. D., Mailhot, J., Bomar, D., Ritzema, E., & Sinclair-Wolcott, C. (Eds.), *DIY Bible Study* (Bellingham: Lexham Press, 2014).

Carr, G. Lloyd, *The Song of Solomon,* Tynbdale Old Testament Commentaries (Downers Grove: Inter-Varsity Press, 1984).

Fox, Michael V., *The Song of Songs and the Ancient Egyptian Love Songs* (Madison: The University of Wisconsin Press, 1985).

Fruchtenbaum, Arnold G., *Biblical Lovemaking* (Tustin: Ariel Ministries Press, 2003).

Garrett, D. A. (1998). The Poetic and Wisdom Books. In D. S. Dockery (Ed.), *Holman concise Bible commentary* (Nashville: Broadman & Holman Publishers, 1998).

Garrett, D. A., *Proverbs, Ecclesiastes, Song of Songs,* The New American Commentary Vol. 14 (Nashville: Broadman & Holman Publishers, 1993).

Glickman, Craig, *Solomon's Song of Love* (West Monroe: Howard Publishing Co., 2004).

Hess, Richard S., *Song of Songs,* Baker Commentary on the Old Testament Wisdom and Psalms (Grand Rapids: Baker Academic, 2005).

Jones, C. M., Song of Songs, Book of, Critical Issues. In J. D. Barry, D. Bomar, D. R. Brown, R. Klippenstein, D. Mangum, C. Sinclair Wolcott, ... W. Widder (Eds.), *The Lexham Bible Dictionary* (Bellingham: Lexham Press, 2015).

Lucas, E., *Exploring the Old Testament: The Psalms and Wisdom Literature* (London: Society for Promoting Christian Knowledge, 2003).

Nelson, Tommy, *The Book of Romance* (Nashville: Thomas Nelson, Inc., 1998).

Ogden, G. S., & Zogbo, L., *A handbook on the Song of Songs* (New York: United Bible Societies, 1998).

Simpson, William Kelly, *The Literature of Ancient Egypt* (London: Yale University Press, 2003).

Water, M., *Bible Teachings Made Easy* (Alresford, Hampshire: John Hunt Publishers Ltd., 1998).

# About the Author

HUTSON SMELLEY is an attorney and Bible teacher residing in Houston, Texas with his wife and six children. He holds advanced degrees in mathematics, law and Biblical studies. He can be contacted at proclaimtheword@me.com.

www.proclaimtheword.me